LUCK

By

John Perreault

Kulchur Press   New York

LUCK

By John Perreault

Published by Kulchur Press

888 Park Avenue, New York, N. Y. 10021

Distributed by Citadel Press

222 Park Avenue South, New York, N.Y. 10003

To whom all orders should be directed.

Library of Congress Catalog Card No. 70-75177

Printed in the U.S.A. By Harry Gantt, New York N.Y. 10040

ACKNOWLEDGEMENTS

Some of these poems have appeared previously in the following magazines:

C, The World, Art and Literature, Locus Solus, Paris Review, Chelsea,

Extensions, 0 to 9, Angel Hair, Mother, Nomad, Tri-Quarterly, Intransit,

Nadada, and Bones. Some have also appeared in the following anthologies:

The American Literary Anthology (Farrar, Straus & Giroux) and The

Young American Poets (Follett).

CONTENTS

THE HOUSEBOAT STRIP

"To pump this heavenly goosebump summer
dry of its squash railroads
and its two left feet,
in an airfield fog as thick as tweed suits
or greenhouse flowers,"

says Gladys who is dressed in her floral dress
on the sundeck of my high-speed houseboat
following tides,

"I stomach your houseboat that doesn't suit me
in which some brand new questions are required
for the slick sponge

or an archery, carefully smooth,
that blends both arrow and target
for the tailgate,
                    swallowing crime."

And I, the owner of this boat,
I lie dreaming on an unmade bed

while airplanes piloted by five o'clock shadows
dip and dive
against the cool sky

spelling out
rimed messages.

"I dump these carloads of waste
off soft shoulders into the mush
where all good children go
who have been seduced by the thumb,"

says Hank, my buddy,
who is opposed to the production of arms
and who is capable of barnstorming
and who is capable of big red barns.

Gratuitously,
timepiece bandstands dissolve around
he-man posture postcards,
imitating luck

while I attempt to become the evening's
blackout fixtures,
a colony of ants
a mixture of these mixtures.

I pull my famous cloud routine
and invest myself in wharfs.

For even the roof of this house has a mouth
or a number of mouths
with which to speak,
                    secretly,
of the pleasures of indifference
or of connection

and with which to seek
the worms as big as summer storms
in the middle of August
                    on someone's thirtieth birthday,
shoveling Dutch.

"In refrigerator compartments
over bedsteads and departments,
kneeling too close to the edge,
badland landlords drop on trolleys

verbal parlays,
obvious naps,
and crisp, white homes,"

says Charlie, my cave,
my brand with a scar on his hand
and a mouse of a pet
in his dream of the prison break
that he and I were inspired to make.

But the planets, my favorites,
alone at last,
after much debate during a caucus
vote an indulgence

                 for those less fortunate
in which

        ————or at least so the headline
        in the Monday N.Y. Times reports————
an outrageous section of the anatomy
fills out cargoes.

It is a thumb as big as the planet Venus.
It is the hollow behind the knee
of a blue crook as he breaks through the glass
of my glass skyway department.

It is a thumb as big as Niagara
and a thumb as big as the gin rummy game
I played to save my life that time on your island,
going for broke.

Telephone booths become voting booths
filled to the brim

or they become shower rooms,
cloudy with steam
and alive with the pressures of touch

————real time as opposed to, supposedly,
ideal motion.

But the fires have already reached this place
and erased all traces
of the geography equipment.
Even the leaf that falls from your tree
and even the grief that smashes
my unsmashable field

has ornaments to announce fluidity
as it circulates within
opaque curtains of lucidity!

In the beginning
there were miles and miles of uglies
and small Greek batallions
that smelled of onions.

To the right of this,
                    next to the shove,
here were rusty cans,
and small agonies
                    the size of landslides.

                              ("In elevator incinerator rooms
                              over reading the lamps and muscle romps,
                              shielding the shape of the land,
                              mailmen tugging ramps hold pow-wows and
                              spill on the rug battery cells,
                              stopwatches — already stopped —
                              and alternate choices,"

                              reads the footnote in a book I am reading
                              on my birthday on the sundeck of my houseboat
                              sailing down the brown Potomac.)

Is it true that the lifeboat was of magnesium?
Were there really visitors from the mid-west
filling out the ranks?
Am I the legal owner of this boat?

Thus it is that avalanche control becomes overt
in high places,
                    overlooking the wife.

Gladys: Overlooking the delicious leftovers
             ——spoons, harps, cheese and grub——
         in the refrigerator in the glove compartment
         that is loaded with fur.

Hank: Overlooking the back issues of Look Magazine
         that contain in endless installments,
         the installments of your flimsey life
             ——your garbage truck syndicate,
         your rise to fame as a fence

or a purveyor of stolen goods,
a movie star in "family" movies,
an opera singer (soprano),
a Jet Set ringleader of wife-swappers,
wife-whippers,
and your unnatural relationships,
with presidents of large armaments corporations
and a former president of the U.S.A.

Wanda: Overlooking the lookout towers shaped like
a fake idea of espionage
that surrounds our head-hunting party
as we search for the wreck.

I am looking over an old copy of Look
when I see,
sandwiched between an ad for telephones
the size of toothbrush nozzles
and a full page peanut butter sandwich
a picture of my Third World War roomate
in the form of an oldster wheeling a baby carriage
across a truck route full of youngsters
wearing holsters

In the distance I am able to see
the tail-end of a noisy parade,
a tailspin
and in the foreground
                    a thumb.

"AN ACHIEVEMENT PACKS ITS BAGS
AND LEAVES THE NIGHT
WITH ALL THE SPOILS
OF A BACKLASH CONTEST,
BEATING THE DARK,"

says the caption, obviously in error
or at least misspelled.

But the captain of my houseboat
interrupts my search for an afidavit
with a long story about his hard life
in the Yukon during the magnesium rush. [1]

Undiminished,
I take off my sparkling white
attempt at a cowboy hat
which is stenciled with the words:
Warehouse Raga Teamplay,
and go for a refreshing dip off the side
of my outboard motorboat.

I like the idea of desolation.
I like the idea of hope.

I even like the idea
of waking up in the morning
in another body
in another place,
completely nude,
pretending I know who I am;

"In downstairs waiting rooms,
over underwear and clear air,
intimates take a shower room
and bend it
and inmates drop on knives

broken railroads,
goat's milk,
flower bedspreads
and broken lives,"

says my Third World War roommate
as he wheels his triplets
down the street
of a small midwestern town,
famous for its annual
dictaphone race

held each year
on the day of my birthday.

I take off my watch,
the strap of which
is stenciled with the words:
Rare Snow,
in order to open the secret compartment
which contains
a compass, a ballpoint pen,
a piece of flint
and three secret messages in code.

1. (Scrawled on the back of a Con Ed bill)

"Old furniture and green hills
snow down on sundown followings
of the gray mind
in its hideout of new furniture." 2

2. (Written in longhand by a lefthanded person)

"Property too upgrades cafeteria wingspans
until the circumstances of these
aria flightplans circumnavigates the gladness
a tragedy of machinery leaves
on its way back home." 3

3. (Typed out on a long piece of tape)

"This damn dam then that values rivers
does not hamper trust,
measuring out friendly mixtures
of quarter-notes and sand,
listing hard knots,

but loosens the stiff control
of quarter-notes and sand,
for the lucky visitors
down where the car park
faces small rooms facing east." 4

Small wonder then that the wanderings
of my after-image
have been recorded by bands
of unequal photographers,
hastening food.

These photographs are elliptical;
these photographs are small.

... Strange mottos of endearment,
zoo balloons,
a seaside afternoon
with umbrellas and sand
and a note for expansion,

and in a dark apartment
or a houseboat
somewhere on the other side of town

a nudity (male) that bends these descriptons
into hair knots
and distant ferris wheels (female),
indicating noon.

I like the idea of photography.
I like the idea of food.

I take off my long back cape
which is stenciled with the words:
Double Glove
and visit a love nest
recently developed,
                    wearing my love nest disguise.

Permanent "lilies" enlighten the "rain"
a square "cloud" drops upon
raw leather "whips"
and the strict manacles
that both "freeedom" and license propose.

No wonder then that
too soon for its own good
a cool room of after thoughts
roams down a hospital hall
that ends in a doll
with eyes the shape of subway tokens.

And all these tokens of deliverance
are an accident of chemistry
a replacement for ropes.

"Minute tendencies to form separate
extensions ...

Minute tendencies to form seperate
extensions
of the exact principle ...

Minute tendencies to form seperate
extensions
of the exact principle
overwhelm major considerations

Minute tendencies to form seperate
extensions
of the exact principle
overwhelm major considerations
of consequence or consistency ..."

repeats the Victrola in the bathroom
of my houseboat, docked,
in behalf of the needle stuck in the scratch
of a special gold record I have made
to promote my talents as a song writer
and my abilities as a rock and roll star.

For your island disappoints me.
It is too wet.
It goes on and on for miles
and then just stops whenever it gets to
the ocean that surrounds us. How come?

How come you keep refusing my presents?
How come you jump to conclusions
too quickly,
trying to pin me down?

A cough takes a picture
that requires a skin test
and then when an "arrow" turns to see
what "plan" it has miraculously survived

it turns out to be a doorway
that leads to a square.

Are there a few live roaches in this pie?
Are there, or will there be, obscenities
behind each wall and around each corner?

Is it true that the bruises are made of magnesium?
That our island of pleasures and displeasures
is made of magnesium, cleverly disguised?

I like the idea of chemistry.
I like the idea of rope.

But the square becomes a circle,
the circle a loop,
and somewhere at the fringes
of this parcel collection,
                              at the starting point,
the troops are restless again
for a gigantic parade. 5

An omission becomes dominant:
these "natures"
(and/or the whole world)
deviate minutely
from the cumbersome!

Your parade consists of ——— (some kind of animal)
and buckets and buckets of
——— (a liquid, any liquid).

Your parade consists of thousands and thousands
of giant movie stars (all your favorites)
stark naked and with braces on their teeth

Your parade consists of appliances and bottles
of Apple Jack
as it turns the corner to follow the jeep.

Your parade consists of a million cheerleaders
wearing short satin skirts
and no underwear,
not even the see-through kind.

Your parade consist of watermelons
and giant flagpoles
bearing the flags of various sex clubs.

But *my* parade, as opposed to *your* parade
consists of two thousand nudists,
aptly displayed.

I take off my orange dinner jacket
that is stenciled with the words
Avalanche.Control
and fold it neatly,
flag-fashion,
and hide it away in my foot-locker.

For my parade consists of topless waitresses
and bottomless waiters
and eleven hundred brands of breakfast food,
hot and cold,

followed by a complete circus
followed by a freak show
followed by eleven hundred species of flowers.

I take off my pale green tie
that is stenciled with the words
Pale Green Tie

and receive my Parade Award, tieless,
in the shade of a missile crisis,
a skyscraper war,
a wrestling match between sculptors and painters.

For my parade consists of foreign aid,
Followed by several skyscrapers on roller skates
half of them vertical like thumbs
and half of them horizontal like guns,
or vice versa
My parade consists of kool-aid and magnesium flares
followed by the nude fashion models of officialdom,
followed by the population of New York City
disguised as me.
And above us the beautiful sky
hangs like a backdrop
dotted with clouds
or airplane motors.

And this sky, which for the past half hour
has been unfolding like a fan
or a road map
                covered with intricate veins
like the palms of my hands,
checks the houseboat sunlamp and the lamp exhibits
a peculiar form of scar tissue
that could be significant
but only to those initiated into the mysteries
of the "historical process." 6

Ocean of my darkest dreams of smooth foliage!
Ocean with airplanes writing out love notes!
Ocean with a face like apple pie!

Fortunately, the "glasses," have been broken
and we are unable to see the false clues
left by remote ancestors,
former tenants
or the friendships 7 that have begun
to weigh down levity
with the tonnage of sincerity.

The sky checks up on the flashlights too
although it is almost completely unnecessary
to the new procedure
that enables us to distinguish
the distant ends of subway platforms
from the distant, but closer
chapters of an unread novel
called *The Great Big Book of Parades*.

"Ocean of my extended winter palace that is like
a forest of the eternally pubic!
Ocean of the Irish seacoast heavy with clams!
Ocean of ups and downs
and pleasantly plump soft hills!"

sings the vanquished pith helmet of my
reclining,
my crimson,
my daffodil itch.

"But these spiritual groceries
flare up vituperously
into housewarmings or post offices,
greeting the host,
envisioning him,
through horn-rimmed glasses,
some sort of sexual robot.
He is, and his double-breasted suit
is impeccable.
He goes around pouring water
into glasses,
always smiling,
always ignoring confrontations,"

sings the hallway of my barometer
signalling trucks
as Gladys does her routine
in the bunkbed
of the galley
photographed by galleries.

"And somewhere near the bottom of the floorplan,
in the middle of the flightplan
a bird eats a spoonful
and changes into a telephone
that refuses to ring,"

sings the pierced earlobe
of my smooth-skinned, houseboat houseboy
as he bails out water from
the houseboat bathtub
springing leaks.
He finds, however, a frame[8]
that divides things up
and makes them, on the one hand,
easier to see
and, on the other hand,
completely invisible.

Is it true that only the telephone was lost
in the previous crack-up?
Or did the lies the "investigator" uncovered
only cover up the loss of my glassware?

It is my thirtieth birthday
on your island of glass
and your island melts.
It folds. It pampers.
It grows a lawn made up of grass
the color of air.

Orange ocean! Houseboat ocean!

*   *   *   *

(Musical Interlude)

"Dark with aboriginal smiles
the uncooked actually plows
rainfields into dust jackets,"[9]

sings Gladys disguised as a plum
on a plate
or the hieroglyphic scratches
on a rusty old skate.

*Sex blames no one. Sex holds
up the curtains and allows
the invisible man to walk
through walls of pleasure and
disbelief.*

"Towering over the hidden supplies
indiginous warts rim
oceanic altitudes
of narrowness and gain
scraping the plunge," 10

sings Hank disguised as a machine
gun factory,
all sections and parts
that is sliding towards
a locked door and a deck of hearts.

*Nevertheless, these truckloads
cannot lug antediluvian sun-
spot designations nature de-
vilishly records deviously in
tree rings.*

"We festoon this image with keepsakes,
———watches that run backwards,
handshakes,
milk-shakes,
piles of unread unreadable books,
and the softness of an empty hallway
scared by enemy occupations," 11

sings Charlie 12 disguised as a magnificent
orange sports car

turning right
and speeding up a one way street
against a traffic light.

And all these footprints, hand-
prints, imprints, lead down
a road that sunlight judicious-
ly records in secret molecules.

"And we evoke the housing development
on a goat that rides
dressed in a second-hand-coat
triumphantly into a line-up
supervised by tough women
opening knee zones
with their northwest camping equipment
strangely colored blue,
in this blue meridian," 13

sings Charlie once again
but this time disguised
as the lower half of an airplane wing
as he swings from the lamp post
of the dock where our houseboat
is docked in our wait for the sun.

And towards a new teleology
of ecology hot sparks irridiate
loosely sexual puns, teasing
the ring-fingers of a wayward
biology.

"Birth bumps head-on into death
and death stands up
only to be knocked down again
by a bus on a highway," 14

sings the Captain who is disguised
as a marmelade sandwich
as he floats down the screen
of a home movie made from press clippings
and tries to keep his fingers clean.

And these so-called photographic armspans repeat the orange armbands worn by cold nudes to elude the efficiency of dexterous gland experts who are teasing the war.

"Hired madmen, dressed to kill,
suck magicians of the wingspan,
hemming and hawing
and eventually sawing them
into triumphant quarternotes
while an all too succulant sunrise
alleviates the waiting line
for rendezvous instructions," 15

sings Wanda Smith, disguised as a teenager,
as she waits for the 2 o'clock bus
and she comes home sailing to us
where we wait for the ages
and are turning the pages
of a novel impossible to kill.

Intoxicated puppeteers of inferior cruelty ovulate airplane tubes narcoleptically manipulating siren news concerts.

"And all these overt aviation explanations
of ineptitude and hate
capture the sunlit roofs of
neighboring but impenetrable
harems,

dropping their weight
into abandoned grain elevators," 16

sings the "vanquished pith helmet,"
the "hallway of my barometer"
and the "pierced earlobe,"

sings a chorus of all of these
and Gladys and Hank and Charlie
and our loveable Wanda.

*   *   *

Orange Ocean! Houseboat ocean!
Star-pimple ocean with radio earphones!

Ocean with a soft legion of legends
and whispered pornography of showmanship!

I take off my handmade shirt
that is made of silk
and that is stenciled with the words
AM/FM Bandstand
and dive into the beer swimming pool
to escape the curve of Hilda's
sexy knee

that has exposed her true mission
once and for all
and has destroyed our houseboat's repose.

And Hank, although he is older,
reminds me of my brother
killed in the magnesium wars
who in turn reminds me of
my Third World War roommate [17]
who reminds me of you.

You and your island made of shellac
and large sheets of music
and crumpled bedsheets,
populated thickly
with the dead children of our love-making.

In the beginning
there were thousands and thousands of trifles
and small Australian armadas
that smelled of encheladas.

To the left of this,
                    next to the cave,
there were soggy pies
the size of pizza pies
and small white tortures
                    the size of bulldozers.

Did Gladys really capture the Mole Fruit
single handedly that night in Rio?
Did Hank who was Charlie's oldest friend
behave in a manner that was surprising to all?
Does Hank still make fun of those less
fortunate
           or more gifted?
Does the Captain of my houseboat
really have a sense of narrative?
Did Wanda dent the bus?

But the Captain can no longer be silenced.
So he treats us to a repeat
of his Magnesium Rush Saga
in a version slightly expanded. 18

Meanwhile we leaf through Hilda's novel 19
which is called *The Great Big Book of Parades*
and we come upon still yet another parade.

It is Gladys' parade.

Gladys' parade consists of
1. several truckloads of armadillos.
2. an iron curtain.
3. various examples of bi-lateral symmetry.
4. numerous floats representing
   the history of the U.S.A.,
   the arms race,
   and various sex positions,
   all executed in tiny rosebuds
   of various shades of pink and red.

And I take off my ordinary cotton T-shirt
which is stenciled with the words
Gazebo Control,
exposing my love wounds
to the crowds assembled on both sides of the street
to witness the finals of the Parade Contest.

I dive into the amplification system
and win back control
of my holdings in the
Magnesium Holding Company
after a fight with my new wife,
Wanda,
about the dispersment of our raft.

I take off my shoelaces
which are stenciled with the words
Cape Cod
and take a nap on my thirtieth birthday
in which I dream of locations
that are pictorial,
islands in a white sea,
handcuffs and typewriter ribbons.

I like the idea of amplification.
I like the idea of marriage.

And I like dreaming on an unmade bed
of a long bus trip
made with cameras
through jungles of popular music.

Picture a man like yourself
stripped to the waist
asleep in a waiting room.

Picture yourself outside a bus station
signaling for fame.

Picture a feature length motion picture
that begins with an envelope

and then ends with a plan
and then ends, almost fortuitously,
with a full grown man.

The Fly-in Drive-in movie theater
is showing a movie
of a slow motion diving board,
scuba divers,
and a documentary diving bell.

These movies are reversed.
These cars, all lined up in a semi-circle,
are empty.
And even this projection booth is empty.

Picture yourself on the deck of houseboat,
completely nude,
as the houseboat is lifted by a crane
onto a flatcar and then onto a boat.

Your island has a hole in it.
And so does your lukewarm parade.
This hole expand and contracts.
The other one eats.

In prevention houselots of small retirements,
over brain stew and the pale squirt,
repairing the rewards of this plan,
ad-men drop on scar tissue

anal hardware,
apple nose-jobs,
and boxes of hard candy.

Adventurously, in pith helmets,
dream aviators become quite nervous
at the sight of
roots they have unearthed
in specific backyards,
instantly cool.

"vehicles[20] of resistence[21]
speed[22] through the speech[23]
on[24] the platform[25] of the extreme   middle[26]
lifting[27] the sledge[28],"

says my houseboy carrying
the black and orange triangular flag
in Hank's parade
that consists of the colors black and orange.

But between these chapters————three and four————
of *The Great Big Book of Parades*
the mailman comes with my mail.

"You wander about in your towel,
amused by the spectacle
of pedants without their spectacles,
opening cocpits
or broom closets,

nailing up the darkness
that is sordid
with the odor of weak berries.

You suppose that this parade,
my favorite,
is not at all what it has so far seemed
————a landscape full of loopholes
or of plums,
a seascape full of plots.

You cut these roots into pungent pieces
and distribute them by mail.

And then when the time is available,
at midnight
pry these windows open
and let the mouths come in.

You stand on the side of the road
with a thumb held out.

A flower grows from that
big fat thumb of yours.

And then when you answer the door
it will only be the mailman again
delivering a package again
once again to the wrong address.

Spring air enters all the windows
of this cross-country Greyhound bus
making the driver (one of your agents)
blush
whenever we pass a clump of flowers
or a particularly attractive hitchhiker.

You monster, you.

You have removed all the seats
and replaced them with raw hot dogs
allowing thereby
abstract dance interpretations
of the darkness found
inside of pocket suit coats.

                    Love,
                         W-A-N-D-A."

Beautiful vague ocean with your pants down!
Pure purple of the unwholesome!
Ocean with your arms full of money!
I take off my right shoe
which is stenciled with the words
Variety Snapdragon
and throw it into the Potomac.

I take off my left shoe
which is stenciled with the words
Cream Cheese Sandwich
and jump into the swimming pool
of Charlie's enormously well-constructed

and consistent parade
that consists of swimming pools
of various shapes and colors,
some floating, some crawling
and some propelled by small atomic reactors.

The first page in the scrapbook
at the bottom of the swimming pool
is a snapshot of Wanda on the brink
of the Grand Canyon,
at sunset.
She is reading my telegram to her
which was in answer to her letter.

"YOUR HARD GARDENS OF APPETITE CONTROL
CAN RAMBLE SEDATELY
THROUGH FOREST FIRES OR ZOO PICNICS
UNBURDENED OF THEIR CANNABALISM
AND STILL NOT BE TOUCHED
BY REALITY, *THE* REALITY
OF INVASION STATISTICS
OR THE SEX LIFE
OF THOSE WHO ARE DISGUISED
AS A DESIRE FOR LINGUISTICS."

Completely cool
she turns to the TV cameras
and begins to sing 29:

> "All my travelings are most with spite
> held openly in a clenched fist,
>
> extracting the soft tooth
> a memory leaves out in the open, unprotected,
> In a public place."

CLOSE-UP OF   *In the beginning there were*
A LARGE TEAR   *thousands and thousand of rifles*
                               and raw Armenian hammocks
                               full of uncooked stomachs.

To the right of this
                    next to the pavement
there were large thumbs
the size of elephant or rhino thumbs
and small fortunes
                    the size of cathedrals.

MIDDLE SHOT OF WANDA   But buried somewhere inside
CUTTING HER PIGTAILS   the elaborate mechanisms
OFF   of the telephone company's
                       equipment center,

                       buried in the syntax of this speech,
                       alive with nouns and commas,
CLOSE-UPS OF WANDA   alive with verbs,
REVEALING HER CROW'S
FEET, HER FROG'S LEGS,   there are orchards hidden by top coats
HER COW'S HIPS, AND   that activate the plummage
HER NERVOUS TIC   that releases the sound
                       at the beginning of each day,

MIDDLE SHOT OF WANDA
AND THE GRAND CANYON
ZOOM TO CLOSE UP OF   and images of jagged seacoasts,
HER SOFT MOUTH   onions within onions,
ABNORMALLY PURPLE   and the nightfall fingering dust."

APPLAUSE

WANDA JUMPS INTO THE GRAND CANYON.
HER PARACHUTE OPENS....

Your island bumps into my island
and the lightning strikes twice
as your island temporarily vanishes.

Crashing sky! Parachute infested
lonely sky
over our houseboat
as we drift away down the brown Potomac!

Why are there wild dogs to greet us
when we arrive near the capital of our daydreams?

Did Gladys plan this or did Hilda?
Was the risk worth taking?
How many hairs do you have on your one good leg?

"Cold cuts (bay rum), several (seven)
days old,
hang (as in 'I'll be hanged')
from the bayonets (bassinets)
at the end (82) of stairways
that twist (beware!) towards the temple
(bank vault) of the clenched fist,
the twisted (loveable) mouth (Wanda's)
in a morphology (mythology)
of stains (fingerprints),"

says our houseboat captain as the news coverage
switches to the Parade Contest
which he has entered with his
prize-winning magnesium statue parade.

Each statue is really a hypnotized person
coated with magnesium
and each statue illustrates
a different stanza of his Magnesium Rush Saga[30]
which is recited over the loud speaker system
to the tune of the state song of Alaska.
Time rescues fortune from the torture room
of the dynamite factory
but fortune refuses to leave
the comfort of its trance.[31]

I like the idea of magnesium.
I like the idea of parade contests.

The second page in the swimming pool scrapbook
which some scholars now think
was intended at one time
to illustrate Hilda Smith's *The Great Big Book of Parades*
is made up of a number of pictures of Hank,

my Third World War roommate
who is the father of Hank the bio-chemist,
Hank the hitchhike member of our gang.

In the *first picture* of a number of pictures
there he is on the side of the highway
that leads to Albany
holding out his thumb.

His thumb looks to be the size
of a baseball bat
but this is only an error caused
by the cheap camera used by Hilda,
a double exposure
or some such trick of the flatness.32

The *second picture* of Hank Sr.
is like the dead body of
someone else's childhood,
a vista of marooned whales
and a wartime town of girlie shows
smoldering in the increased heat
where only slick lizards
are available
for the coming famine.

But where is Hank in this picture?
Where is his sweet, rough face
that is so much like a stovepipe?

On the trunk of a tree on the left
next to the rain barrel
and the wheelbarrow
carved in capital letters
are the words to our
favorite song:

SCAR TISSUE HAS BEGUN TO FORM
AT THE EXACT POINT OF PENETRATION
EVENTUALLY TO LEAVE

A HALF MOON UNDER THE LEFT RIB
SIGNIFYING

AN ADVANCEMENT OF BAD MANNERS,
A TOSS OF THE COIN,
A CHANGE IN DIRECTIONS.

The *third picture* is called
"Life likes the idea of solitary confinement
and life likes the idea of publicity,"

for it shows Hank naked
standing in the middle of a green lawn.[33]

The sky is a peculiar
shade of brown
somewhat like a woman's pocketbook.

But this oddly colored sky
hovers like a vacuum cleaner,

emptying half-notes, quarter notes
and   whole-notes

as that body,
                over there in the houseboat kitchen
drinking coffee,
                fills up
cubicals of misused time.

Hank's thumb which is as big as
Charlie's smaller one
or as big as all of Gladys
lifts up its head, opens its lips
and says quite clearly in French:

            "Paranoia flowerpots fall from
            the houseboat fire escape

            and down by the river
            a car pulls up,

lets off steam,
and a passenger gets out,
shoeless, shirtless,
hatless, and   wearing white trousers."

The *fourth and final picture* of Hank
is a snapshot of Hank lying on an unmade bed;
in his right hand there is a flower,
in his left a gun.

Time becomes an incline of short steps
nude bodies make in elevators
to the climax of
metronomes
and synthetic Saskatchewans.

Inclinations become destinations
and numerical coefficients
hold out thumbs.

Truck drivers, on the other hand,
complement the implements by force,
heeding only the streaming headlights
that illuminate the dreamy faces
of ambitious young hitchhikers.

But the past is much to dangerous to speak to,
to touch,
to approach with tuning forks
or the peculiar instruments
held out gingerly
to the blue-green glare.
So just in the knick of time
the immediate future arrives
in the form of a motorcade
all decked out
with streamers and flags.

This future is a picture of Hank's son

Hank
when he accidently bumps into the secret plan
I have to control the inland waterways.

The present, however, is a parade, Hank's,
that consists of envelopes and Sam,[34]
cowboys and Indians,
the state of Indiana,
the country of India,
and tubs of India ink.

In a distant blur in this picture
I am making an acceptance speech to my constituents
which, if my memory serves me,
goes over quite well
and ends like this:

"The theme you see, is the same as
its infinite variations
holding back the release of
the epicyclic train of ideas
a mind spins out
equating violence with restraint.

"Violence, in itself, is cyclical
and affords no new espousements,
no new angles,
of the chord structures
which have been added
by Icelandic aviaries
to the dictionaries old men dimly grope."

Have we all been followed,
at one time or another?
Will Hilda ever catch up with Wanda?
What color is the center of your island?

I like the idea of islands.
I like the idea of violence.

So picture a gang bang.
Picture a gag.

Picture a small man who hardly
ever leaves his houseboat
and spends his mornings drinking coffee,
answering phones.

Picture a lesson in geography
drawn out into infinity
on the wrong map.

Picture an end-stop, a short-stop,
a dead-end street
with a beautiful door.

The ceiling changes places
with the floor;
wall sockets pour out water
watering the grass
that grows up between the floorboards.

I take off my socks which are stenciled
with the words
Rear Admiral
and jump into the gun.

The houseboat becomes a showboat,
temporarily,
and to the left of the stage
a sign announces:

    *   *   *   *   *   *   *   *   *

        Vaudeville Stool Pigeons
*   Perform Their Act   *
        Attached To The Inept Bordello
*   In A Small Hut   *
        Constructed Upon Principles Of Division
*   And On Numerical Exceptions   *
        To the Whims Of The Majority!!!
    *   *   *   *   *   *   *   *   *

GLADYS (wearing a white cowboy hat)

Your aviation levitations
have traveled along the armed highway
inching testicles of New Mexico
off the dreamy roadbed
into touch and go lunchrooms of touch!

CHORUS

Ocean of your darkest dreams of smoots foliage!

CHARLIE (wearing a long black cape)

Your network of surprise radiance
makes new maps that reveal
the crossroads and turn-offs
most likely to yield
a view of the field!

CHORUS

Ocean of the Irish seacoast heavy with clams!

THE CAPTAIN (wearing an orange dinner jacket)

Your trick mirrors mirror truck farms
that heave themselves into
evasions of the warm fluid
Minneapolis tries to hide
inside its vanishing metropolis!

CHORUS

Orange ocean! Houseboat ocean!

AUTHOR

But the theme returns again
and this time it is disguised as
a unique way of looking out of

windows
or out of mirrors.

Sex jumps the gun
and

indistinguishable from
love
or perception

clears the air
for elaborate deliberations
on the problems of the stop-gap,
the over lap,
the step-up,
overpopulation
or survival!

CHORUS

Beautiful vague ocean with your pants down!

HANK JR. (wearing a pale green tie)

Well-deliberated
avenues of deliverance
once thought pure

are now quite over-grown
with thorns
and wild animals
hunting for mates!

CHORUS

Ocean with your arms full of money!

YOU (wearing shoelaces)

Apprentice butchers hang their handicraft
majestically upon the TV station's

radio causeway,
integrating beauty treatments
with impudent Indian call boys.
who are as tender as the thumb
that I hammer into the motors
that the harmless chases
through systems of nylon!

CHORUS

Crashing ocean!

AUTHOR

And your thumb becomes a roadsign,
a flag,
a lightning rod
a signal for crime.

Your thumb becomes my island,
a tree,
a radio station,
or a very long whip!

He takes off his white trousers
And then he takes off his underwear
which is stenciled with the words
Triumphant Houseboat
And he jumps into the volcano,
Pursued by Hilda.

I like the idea of houseboats!
I like the idea of nudity!

CHORUS

Beautiful ocean of armpits and parachutes!
Ocean of flowers and parade floats!

HILDA (wearing white trousers)

My love turned itself inside out
and became a huge tractor
equipped with interlocking fingers.

Asking questions of these freeways
and these movements on the board,
a moment actualizes the sweet vocabularies
of August's birthday brainstorm

and a smile for the sweetness
a strangeness plants
on the face of the vernacular.

For the stomach has reasons all its own,
empirical saturation points,
myopic vocal chords,
and a lust for the small, soft pleasures
that grow up hard enough to eat
or release
or please with a speech.

> *CHORUS* (in the form of a parade)

Beautiful ocean of armpits and parachutes!
O ocean of flowers and parade floats!

THE END

1. *"Total darkness for days on end.*
I was dazed. I was mad with lust.
And then we stumbled into
the camp of a band of outlaws,
fumbled about in the general chaos,
took our stand.
My hips were badly bruised in the rigged elections.
There were pirated editions and stovepipes everywhere
Few of us remained. I killed him.
How could I forgive him?
The Eskimos were friendly.
Finally after a long truce H
and several unbelievable combats . . ."

2. *Vehicles of resistence*
shall speed through the speech
on the platform of the extreme middle
lifting the sledge.

3. *Cold cuts, several days old,*
shall hang from the bayonets
at the end of a stairway
that twists towards the temple
of the clenched fist,
the twisted mouth,
in a morphology of strains.

4. *Vaudeville stool pigeons*
shall perform their act
attached to the inept bordello
in a small hut
constructed upon principles of division
and on numerical exceptions
to the whims of the majority.

5. *"For it is, in the last analysis,*
an evasion of crime,
that disrupts the war
or a carton of postcards
cleverly phrased
that delivers our city
from the carnivorous siege" . . . . Radio broadcast.

6. *See Appendix I*

7. *Gladys—a dwarf who loves hoop skirts*
and who is inclined to melancholia.

   Hank—a bio-chemist added to the retinue
   while hitchhiking on a Sunday,
   never suspecting the evil
   kidnapping plan he would be party to.

   Charlie—a truck driver.

   The Captain—an old man with a false memory
   and a narrative style that is not exactly
   lucid or relevant

   Wanda—a famous registered nurse,
   who was once a famous opera singer
   and/or a concert pianist
   and who is missing one thumb.

Hilda—(not yet introduced)
is Wanda's mother, madly in pursuit
of her wayward star-struck daughter
whose thirst for adventure
is only matched by her mother's (Hilda's)
lust for revenge.
Houseboy—(not yet introduced)
came with the houseboat and cannot speak.
Houseboat—a barge from the Erie Canal
fitted out with a trailer truck,
a trailer,
a swimming pool,
and a pale blue TV screen.

8. *See Appendix II*
9. *to the tune of Parade Rest Rock.*
10. *to the tune of the aria from Biondo's opera Balloon Parade*
11. *to the tune of I Love A Parade.*
12. *See Appendix III*
13. *to the tune of I Am Parade from Burton's Parade Suite.*
14. *To the tune of the second theme from Okulski's Symphony #12 ("The Parade").*
15. *To the tune of Easter Parade.*
16. *To the tune of I Love A Parade.*
17. *In the bottom drawer of my desk*
    I keep a snapshot of your shot-put
    and a snapshot of your dog.
    I keep a record and a recording
    of your foibles
    on an LP recording of your snore
    interrupted by the dream talk
    that has been so influential
    and has opened up new vistas
    for my brand new lecture series.
18. *See Appendix IV*
19. *Now, unfortunately, out of print.*
20. *Model-T Fords*
21. *"elephants"*
22. *as in Ahead*
23. *"Variety must enter in the form of*
    an exciting uniformity,
    comforting the slow drip
    or a roof leak
    and a proof that needs no proving . . ."
24. *"on" as opposed to "off" as in "off his rocker."*
25. *"Sex blazes a trail*
    hands leave on their way
    to hot epidemics of word games,
    mapping exoteric regions of
    ectoplasm and/or
    actions more passionate
    than narrative . . ."
26. *middle*
27. *about two inches*
28. *a vehicle mounted on runners, and of various forms, used for traveling over snow and ice, as in northern countries.*
29. *To the tune of O My Parade!*

30. *See Appendix IV*
31. *And it is only within these dangerous waters*
   that a line can be drawn
   between that which is pleasant
   and that which is necessary.

   It is only within these stormclouds
   that a tendency to sing
   can delineate itself
   and alleviate the painful.

   Halfway down the ladder of these inland lakes
   making an electricity
   that moves like a houseboat
   through cages of elasticity,

   adventure, therefore, clings to hills
   the way a lost animal
   attaches itself to any convenient
   warmth,
   sucking its thumb.
32. *"You publish a gun.*
   You publish an infamous memoir
   in a mirror old men have purchased
   for their beautiful sons,"
   says Hank as the cars whizz by.

   "You wander around in a get-up
   designed by a whim
   that somebody sneaked past
   the elaborate precautions.

   "You wander about in your skin
   testing this and that,
   trying to determine if these pictures left behind
   are sweet enough or real."
33. *The lawn only looks gray*
   because the picture is a black and white snapshot
   but Hilda remembers quite clearly
   the greenness of the lawn
   and that it was the lawn behind the house
   that Gladys built
   with the money from the war.
34. *Hank's dog.*

APPENDICIES

Appendix I: The Historical Process

The "historical process" begins as a small tube
attached to the left ventrical.
From here it joins the mainstream with a series
of by-products
connected to the main shaft
by a system of interlocking wheels.

This temperance causes the temperature
to rise
halfway up the spinal column,
disguising the chosen

as it reaches for
still further melodic incongruities.

Here, therefore, somewhere, not yet the middle,
a house burns down
and a hole opens up.

Real time becomes imaginary ice roadblocks
that hurl the hourly imitation
of trailer camps and trailer trucks
into floral intervals.

Volunteer firetrucks escape the smoke
a logician makes
rapidly
with a piece at a time.

Good news, however, hovers
like an angel of deliverance
over the turbulance.

It comes and goes. It investigates
the secret passageways of a continent
and accidently locates
the splendors of the thoroughly ordinary.

The "historical process" ends as it began
in an explosion
detached from the world trade centers,
joining up with, as it were,
the expanded nerve centers
where, through a simplicity of gears
or a light network,
it is short-circuited by an interior view
not necessarily sacred,
not necessarily secular.

Tremendous sunspots
dictate tender disruptions
hardly visible
that cause

elastic roadways
to mimic looseness in the shape of
causeways,
engaging the flame.

Appendix II: The Frame Problem

Confronting the frame problem
is like confronting a mirror
of hindsight that reflects
upon itself

and creates,
               within its boundaries,
whole universes within
this "framed" universe,

opening pools of visibility
that contradict
the divisions of the spacious.

And inside the frame
a cow makes love to a tractor,
plants bloom,
a man gets off an airplane
and lands in a tree.

Inside the frame,
a man, a women, and a little boy
are engaged
in rearranging continents.

Inside the frame,
a houseboat becomes a museum
of loose ends, calendar landscapes,
telephone calls.

For a game is a system of instructions,
a universe in miniature
that summarizes, horizontally

vertical shifts in musical structure,
overlapping the turnstiles
and all possibilities
within a given set of determinates.

Outside the frame,
temporarily off the beaten track
I wander around.
I go for a walk by the river
They take me to their hideout in New Jersey,
and am accosted by thugs.
a cabin,
and tie me to a bed with a brass bedstead.
I like them. They like me.
We get along famously.

For a game is an elaborate system of defense
that works out well
as long as everyone can figure out the rules,
can count on the rules,
and agrees with them.

This smallness is the largest form
of deception
possible to the environment:
a few bent twigs,
a stone,
and someone sunbathing.

These magnificent trees, for instance,
in a forest of "X" dimensions,
hemmed in by milestones
eclipse the destinies
of the smaller,

moving their roots,
intermittantly by brainstorms.

Appendix III: Charlie

"Famous cowhands hand me the soap
through the portholes
longevity makes
as it reaches for my steady.

Borrowed for the moment,
I sink to the tip
of a peculiar mountain
my truck passed by
as it careened to the left
of where I left
when I signed the contract,
negotiating pills.

Gas stations   forever tempt me
with their inconsequential Coke machines
and their sanitary washroom keys.

Brinksmanship and brakesmanship
hold hands as I doze
and my two cold hands
tune radios in rainbow colors
as I speed through dreamy intersections.

Careful abortions, slot machines,
and all the high gear of interstate
balance systems

follow me to all-nite diners
where my waitress nods
and thanks me with a monkey dish
of slaw or Boston beans
to relinquish the hold I have
on her law with the boss.

Clean me! Dawn's superhighway
carefully cuts

my unearthly planet into
two equal right-angle triangles.

And gas stations forever tempt me
with all their lubrication paraphernalia.

My sidekick groans.
My pale boots. My mud. My wife back home.
And when I step from the telephone booth
my truck, as it pulls away from the warehouse
loading platform,
is loaded up
with pieces of thumb."

Appendix IV: The Magnesium Rush Saga

"Total darkness for days on end and at the center
a coolness that was creepy.
I was dazed. I was mad with lust.
Alaskan avenues of discourse
opened up into highways of Alaskan surprise
and horticulture developed a need
for blood samples.

Afterwards, the tree that bleeds,
during the course of a routine investigation
concerning the whereabouts of the hideout,
brought the roustabouts a booby-trap,
a sandwich,
to their concealed stockade.

And then we stumbled into
the camp of a band of outlaws,
fumbled about in the general chaos,
took our stand,
and a bird flew out of a brand new cage.

Up there above the imperial targets,
up there above the billboards
and the outposts,
it captured a few lost memories.

But my hips were badly bruised in the rigged elections.
so of course, during the course of
this so-called routine investigation
airplanes broke loose from their strings
and bombed an Alaskan rosebush factory
spilling their seeds
all over the source of our misery.

There were pirated editions and stovepipes everywhere.
Explorers, like myself,

of this ornate jungle
that hides inside these objects
or these sentences
soon found themselves deleriously afraid.

·Few of us remained. I killed him.
An Alaskan photographer
had removed all the seats
from the balcony of an imaginary movie house
and thereby made possible
deliberate field games
played with telephone books
and all the trappings
of theater wings and office equipment.

How could I forgive him?
There on the roadside
next to the roadsign
my thumb became a paint brush
or a ballpoint pen
tracing out
an enigma of equilateral triangles.

The Eskimos were friendly
and trim uniforms increased the uniformity
in this house on wheels
easing the disparity
a wigwam has
as it eclipses the hoax.

Finally after a long truce
and several unbelievable combats,
velvet lofts in districts
slightly out of sight
violate steamrooms
hidden from
popular notions of diversity.

And within these rooms,

preserved by a thin layer of film
it was impossible to piece together
the ordinary lives
of the local inhabitants.

The footprints lead to tarpits.
The arrows pointed to a surprise
poised on an upper shelf,
snarling effectively
at the minute geometry.

Finally after a long truce
and several unbelievable combats
variety enters in the form of
an Alaskan magnesium lode,

variety enters in the form of
a neatness
completely detached from the stove.

READYMADES, ETC. [1960-2]

Flag

The Flag of the United States of America has thirteen horizontal stripes ————seven red and six white————the red and white stripes alternating, and a union which consists of white stars of five points on a blue field placed in the upper quarter next to the staff and extending to the lower edge of the fourth red stripe from the top. The number of stars is the same as the number of States in the Union. The Canton or Union now contains fifty stars, each star with one point upward.

The colors of the Flag may be thus explained: The red is for valor, zeal and fervency; the white for hope, purity, cleanliness of life, and rectitude of conduct; the blue, the color of heaven, for reverence to God, loyalty, sincerity, justice and truth.

The star (an ancient symbol of India, Persia and Egypt) symbolizes dominion and sovereignty, as well as lofty aspiration.

The Meaning of Existence

Mr. Moore reports that he once kissed his favorite department store mannequin just to see what it was like. "It was like kissing a desk," he said, but his experience had not affected their relationship.

Ellipse

1. The planets move in elliptical orbits about the sun with the sun at a focus. The earth's orbit is an ellipse.
2. Satellites move in elliptical orbits about planets.
3. The "terminator" of the crescent moon——the curved line separating the bright portion of the moon and the dark portion——is elliptical.
4. The elliptical arch is used in architecture for its beauty. The arches of stone and concrete bridges are frequently semi-ellipses.
5. Elliptical gears are used in machines to obtain a slow, powerful movement with a quick return, as in power punches.
6. Whispering galleries usually have elliptical ceilings arranged so that one may stand at a focus and hear a slight noise made at the other focus, while a person standing between foci hears nothing.
7. In a certain type of map projection, designed to preserve relative area, the meridians become arcs of ellipses.
8. Steam boilers are said to have greatest strength when the heads are elliptical.
9. The area of action of an airplane which leaves a moving carrier and returns in a given time with no wind, is an ellipse.

10 Year Old Girl
Falls Into River
Drowns

A 10 year old girl was drowned last night when she slipped off a rock into 10 feet of water in the Black River near her home.

... Firemen responded with a boat but were unable to use grappling hooks because of rocks in the river.

The girl's mother recently was remarried. She and her husband have three other children: Eileen, 18; Patricia, 11; and James, 13.

Ayand J 2/2 etaoin etaoi e e ceez.......

The Mountains

Do not enter without one or more
companions and do not separate.

Use only regular trails and
avoid all short cuts.

Obey all posted signs.

There should be at least one adult
for every five children.

Watch out for snakes.

Do not enter caves or mine shafts.

Do not roll or throw rocks.

Allow yourself plenty of time to
get out of the mountains
before it gets dark.

If lost or injured, get to high
point or clearing if possible and
remain until help arrives.

Hatbox

The robot, which looks like a huge hatbox on wheels, is the only one in the world that can survive in a natural environment ———— in this case a maze of corridors and offices.

When its 12 batteries start to run down, the Beast feels its way along a corridor until it finds an electrical outlet. When contact is made the robot inserts two prongs into the outlet and recharges the batteries. Then it pulls out the prongs and moves along.

What You Should Do In An Emergency

1. Report situation immediately. Emergency phones are located in the center corridor next to the north elevators.
2. Always note locations of exits and fire escapes. Those are marked by red lights.
3. In case of emergency, or when leaving your room, make sure door is closed.
4. Keep calm——panic is often more dangerous than the emergency.

To Be Or Not To Be

Walter Slezak on sitting behind Elizabeth Taylor in the theater, quoted by Earl Wilson:

> "And she had on long earrings of emerald. Sometimes I could see the stage through the emeralds and do you know, that's a wonderful way to see 'Hamlet'————through emeralds!"

Learning To Speak Tahitian Like A Native

Hello.
Good morning.
How are you?
What's new?

Do you speak English?
I do not understand.
I need an interpreter.
I don't speak Tahitian.

Please speak slowly.
Please repeat.

I am American.
What is your name?

Do you want a drink?
Do you want a cigarette?
May I take your picture?

Show me the way to...
Please let me come with you.
I want to...

Woman.
Man.
White person.

I'm going home.
Let's go!
Come here!
Turn right!
Turn left!
Please take me to your....

Who is this?
What is the name of this?
What is the price of this?

The Lady Receiving Her Visitor

What a noise the boy makes!
What beautiful flowers these are!

*   *   *

There were a dozen handsome trees, and under them
a piece of artificial water where boys were sailing
toy boats, and a poodle was swimming.

*   *   *

Many strange stories were told of this adventure.

*   *   *

Go into the other street.
Do not look for trouble.

*   *   *

The uncouth person in the tattered garments dropped on both knees on
the pavement, and took her hand in his, and kissed it in passionate gra-
titude. He rose, and stood with his cap in hand. She bowed to him, and
passed on, grave and stately. She was an amiable but strictly matter-of-
fact person.

*   *   *

How different the place looked now!

*   *   *

He wrapped his cloak about me.

*   *   *

Come here and sit on my knee.
What is your name?
Can you tell me the road to Denver?

* * *

Phillip, your father is calling.
Phillip, do you own a horse?
Phillip, open the door.
What a fellow you are, Phillip.

* * *

He was lying on a crimson sofa reading a French
novel. It was a very little book. He is a very
little man. In that enormous hall he looked like a mere speck.

* * *

Mr. Ash lives in the next house.

* * *

Each man took a pear.

* * *

How sorry I am!
My friend, here you are!
Here are the dancing bears!

* * *

Swim for your life.
Jump. It's your last chance.

* * *

The lady received her visitor graciously.
The lady received her visitor in a gracious manner.
The lady received her visitor with graciousness.
The lady received her visitor in a gracious fashion.

* * *

Seals are amphibious.

*　*　*

Do I blame the man?
Do you feel better?
Does Charlie work?
Did you find your knife?
Who is on guard?
Whom do you see?
Does Henry skate well?
Do bananas grow in Africa?

The Venus Fly Trap

1) A Beautiful Plant!

Its dark green leaves form a low symmetrical rosette. Each leaf is tipped with a lovely pink trap.

2) Eats Flies And Insects!

Each pink trap contains a bit of nectar. It is this color and sweetness which attracts the unsuspecting insect. Once he enters the trap, it snaps shut. Digestive juices then dissolve him.

3) Eats Flies and Insects!

When the insect has been completely absorbed, the trap reopens and prettily awaits another morsel.

4) A Beautiful Plant!

Traps will bite *at*————but not *off*————"more than they can chew."

5) Feed It Raw Beef!

If there are no insects in your house, you can feed the traps tiny slivers of raw beef. The plant will thrive on such food.

6) Instructive For Children!

Youngsters especially will enjoy growing these exotic plants. And if, somehow, you can convey the thought that many of life's alluring enticements can prove to be traps, you will have made a priceless investment!

7) Easy To Grow!

They thrive in glass containers and develop traps in three to four weeks. They will beautify any room in your house.

Allegories

Using any paperbound dictionary, read aloud in alphabetical order all the words beginning with "a."

Or "b" or "c" or any letter of your own choosing.

This can be done alone or in front of an audience.

Several people using different letters of the alphabet can do this simultaneously either aloud or silently, either for each other or in front of an audience.

Twenty-six people can do this together, each choosing a different letter of the alphabet. When each person is finished reading his section of the dictionary he must leave the room or leave the stage.

Homage To *

Choose any work of fiction. Open the book at random. Only the left-hand page is to be used. The last digit of the page number determines how many of the words of the last line on the page are to be read. Slowly count the number of words before reading them aloud. This will determine silences. If the last digit is "O," count off all of the words in the line, but do not read anything aloud. Continue for any pre-established length of time.

* Insert the name of the author of the book that is being used.

The Name Of This Poem Is*

Choose any work of fiction. Open the book at random. Beginning with
the top line of the page you have opened to, read the first word (or part
of word) at the beginning of each line. Pauses must be made before each
paragraph indentation, but other pauses may be improvised.

When the first page has been read in the above manner, open the book
at random to another page and repeat the same process. Continue this
for any pre-established length of time.

* Insert the name of the book that is being used.

But

Pronounce the word "but" for at least two minutes, improvising pauses, inflection, pitch, changes in volume, etc.

And

The "score" consists of any one page chosen at random from any book.

Beginning at the upper left hand corner of the score, the reader begins counting the words silently, counting repeatedly from one to ten.

The reader pronounces the word "and" one time for each mark of punctuation as he comes to it.

Marriage

A church on a Sunday afternoon. The Minister is facing the congregation (audience). There is a traditional bridal procession with appropriate organ music.

Cast of Characters

The Minister.......... played by a real minister.

The Bride............. played by an actress who will use her own name in the appropriate blank spaces of the following text.

The Groom........... played by an actor who will use his own name in the appropriate blank spaces of the following text.

The Best Man.

The Maid of Honor.

The Bride's Father.

Flower girls and numerous relatives, etc.

(The order of persons before the Minister shall be from left to right as follows: The Best Man, the Groom, the Bride and the Maid of Honor.)

The Minister: Dear Friends: We are gathered here in the presence of of God and before these witnesses, to unite this man and this woman in matrimony. This estate was first instituted of God in the creation of the family, and consecrated by Christ by His presence at the marriage in Cana of Galilee. We thus discover the home and family to be the natural foundation of human society. Therefore marriage should not be entered into unadvisedly or hurriedly, but with due reverence and discretion, and as in the sight of God.

(Addressing the persons to be married.) The motive in your coming here should be love and the building of a home. I therefore charge you before God to preserve these vows which you are about to make, as inviolate. To the measure this is done this union will bring you peace and happiness, and you shall survive every vicissitude of life.

(To the Groom.) ————————, wilt thou take this woman to be thy wedded wife, to live together in the holy estate of matrimony. Wilt thou love her, comfort her, honor and keep her, in sickness and in health; and forsaking all others keep thee only unto her, so long as ye both shall live?

The Groom: I will.

The Minister: (To the Bride.) ————————, will thou take this man to be thy wedded husband, to live together in the holy estate of matrimony. Wilt thou love him, comfort him, honor and keep him, in sickeness and in health; and forsaking all others, keep thee only unto him, so long as ye both shall live?

The Bride: I will.

The Minister: Who giveth this woman to be married to this man?

The Father: I do.

The Minister (taking the hand of the woman from her sponsor and placing it in the hand of the man): Repeat these words after me. I,————————, take thee ————————, to be my wedded wife, to have and to hold, from this day forward, for better, for worse, for richer, for poorer, in sickness and in health, to love and to cherish forever.

The Groom: I, ————————, take thee ————————, to be my wedded wife, to have and to hold, from this day forward, for better, for worse, for richer, for poorer, in sickness and in health, to love and to cherish forever.

The Minister: Repeat after me. I, —————, take thee, —————, to be my wedded husband, to have and to hold, from this day forward, for better, for worse, for richer, for poorer, in sickness and in health, to love and to cherish forever.

The Bride: I, —————, take thee, —————, to be my wedded husband, to have and to hold, from this day forward, for better, for worse, for richer, for poorer, in sickness and in health, to love and to cherish forever.

The Minister (to the Groom): Do you have a ring, a token of this vow?

The Groom: I do.

The Minister (receiving the ring): The wedding ring represents the unbroken bond which now unites these two hearts together in an endless love. You will place this upon your bride's finger saying these words: I take this ring in token of my pledge of love and faithfulness, and as I place it upon your hand I renew my vows before Almighty God.

The Groom (placing ring on the Bride's finger): I take this ring in token of my pledge of love and faithfulness, and as I place it upon your hand I renew my vows before almighty God.

The Minister: Let us pray.... O God, our Father, Builder and Maker of our homes, giver of spiritual grace, teacher of Love: send Thy blessings upon these two, this man and this woman, whom we bless in Thy holy name: that they may surely be true to their promises one to another, and faithfully perform and keep their vows between them made. And may they live together in perfect love and peace and understanding, and obey all Thy laws, through Jesus Christ our Lord. Amen.

Forasmush as ————— and ————— have consented together in holy wedlock, and have witnessed the same before God and these witnesses, and thereto have pledged their faith to one another, and have confirmed the same by joining hands, and by giving and receiving a ring; I therefore declare that they are husband and wife, in the name of the Father, and of the Son, and of the Holy Spirit. Those whom God hath joined together, let no man put asunder. Amen.

(Everyone kneels.) Let us pray: Our Father, who art in heaven: Hallowed be Thy name, Thy Kingdom come, Thy will be done, on earth as it is in heaven. Give us this day our daily bread. And forgive us our trespasses, as we forgive those who trespass against us. And lead us not into temptation, but deliver us from evil. For Thine is the kingdom, and the power, and the glory, forever. Amen.

(Bridal procession exits down center aisle of church. Outside they are showered with rice.)

The End

UNTITLED

Little Egypt

Egypt, my secret, discloses a spy,
nodding significantly
from a sandy roadster that passes by
on a Greek turnpike,

revealing my privacy
in an artificial park behind
libraries of involuntary sadness.

Rosicrucian teamsters
unload the barge
that contains
an outline of the future.

Thusly, each pure sound becomes
at the end of its cone
not completely verbal,

but in its own way
affluent,

melting away at the end of
a sealed vestibule

like a torpedo
that has been tampered with
and left outside.

These so-called enemies of industry
give birth, therefore,
to crates of camel hump
and candied dates
in the floors above
transparent funeral parlors
in a section of Cairo
not usually available to archaeologists.

Oasis appetites climb up from sleep
for the soft flesh
of the imports
grows bronze horns
in the midnight of my quick leap
into your poolside cabana.

A stick becomes a stab in the back
in a moist alley
and an assassin seals my lip
with some liquid from the pyramids
or some tissue paper
found at the foot of the Sphinx.

But you arrive with your squadron,
circumventing the obstacles I have made
in an effort to avoid
the footprints of a mass-murder,

and my exuberant cartwheels become nailed
to a small piece of the sky,
rather pie-shaped,
loosening the tongue of the smallness
that opens the cliff.

You bang your blondness against the swimming pool
and the swimming pool,
my share of the inheritance tax,
swims away into the brown varnish.

Egyptian movie stars
pose on diving boards
too numerous to saw.

Egyptian sunspots focus my view
of the hard light
my eyes keep closing to see.

I open them again
when no one is looking

and you are asleep
on the handgrenade pile of old newsprint,
disguised as The Book of the Dead,
here in these archives
of the decline of the West.

I want to see myself quite clearly
early in the morning of your pregnancy
spending a fortune in rubies
each time you are reflected
from a mirror
propelled by bygone centuries.

I want to see myself
not under the influence
of the Magna Carta
or the steady gaze
of your Italian chauffeur,

for an enclosure of these open doors
can nullify
if I allow it
and if by mistake
I swallow it

car baby carriages that crash into
my top secret information,
my clues to the crop,
my techniques of disguise.

Allowing this push button surprise,
dawn-colored palm trees
isolate a beautiful disease,
amplifying an adjustment of

hot sand and
metaphors of deliberate celibacy
as opposed to the triumph of Angola.

But "equality" characteristically
makes a stalemate
that upsets the equalibrium
of the nude cliff,

illusions of the senses, private
verb-endings,
normal morals,
collisions into softness.

And then from out of nowhere
you cause a tetrahydron
and a liquor-colored liquid
oozes out of this disclosure
perfumed ominously
                    at each acuteness

with an astuteness
and with a diversity of extinct
blue flowers.

I inhale the grammar
of these seeds
that won't quite sprout.

I go out for a long walk
across the desert
where notions of splendor
close out at lower prices,
opening leaks.

Your tent
refuses a slice of my dangerous life,
developing along the shorelines
loopholes
often resembling star loopholes

and each of these rubdowns
performed in your harem
of teenage Arabs

is dangerous,
                    but not contagious,
inches deep,
at last quite numb.

For you are so pointlessly
European in your housedress
and with your dyed blond hair,
spying on me, following me with your horde,
lacking all the open pleasures,
visions of the buried sky,
or poisons that have been rumored to heal
antiquarian star maps.

Engine trouble. Clocks stop.
Clip-joints become undone
and I appear to myself in a dream of
colossal palm trees
fed by bad habits of obedience.

Open tunnels heave forth soup.
Pie becomes an agenda of hoops.
Environments of heat lift heads
to neat openings in the inverse hill,
closing the air vents
I made in the glass.

You have invented these instruments
for my amusement
hoping to trap me,
but when I unwrap them

an hieroglyphic flies out, leaving wingprints,
not fingerprints,
close to all the bathroom fixtures.

Here then dry ice decorates the doors of
a pyramid that floats;
and fashion, that ghost of invention,
eats up novelties
the way you eat up the landscape

as it speeds by the sidecar
of your pearl-white Harley-Davis.

Could this be the reason that
I came here earlier for the burial of
close quarters? Or is this
lateness the answer?

Closer to this outline is further from
rrozen lakes,
vertical on a playing field
like mirror pedestrians
out for a stroll along the Gaza.

This dying therefore, that we have
flirted with so often
over cool drinks on luxury Hilton terraces
becomes an object lesson
I only wish to learn,
if at all,
at a distance of at least ten miles.

And all these darker places praise
an envy of caves
each fraction has as it mounts

camels and horses I draw
from the Egyptian bathtub waves,
aiming them home.

Egyptian magnets open exits
that evolve
northward along the green river,
disconcerting the reeds,

and then the inevitable surprise visit
sidecars bring
                in manila envelopes
to the sluice gates of the Nile.

The Wave

I swallow the pill and the pill
swallows me,
perhaps not completely but it seems
the colors are all white.

Running toward the rim
gone are all the afternoons
I washed the sea,
enclosing the rain.

All the signs seek flowered hats,
lakes without bottoms or names,
landslide commercial displays,
the field.

Goats hold hands with Pontiac rooms
but tomorrow the camels will vanish
into tents of famine
and of hieretical alphabets.

I stomach the evening that's
enclosing the shoe
that pain wears as it stumbles
across the glass lawn.

Down by the shiny gas pump,
staring at the dawn,
tank farmers eat the triangular.

Tortured by pleasures,
an old friend
neatly brings a package
down to the Mohawk River,
seals a letter, sends it,
opens a wall
and nudges a small animal
out of its warm brown sleep.

Why are there icebergs
in my sea
that massively
hamper traffic,
linking the continent of
India with me
by obstacles not tentacles?

Naturally, things change
into things and things go on
at an uneven pace,
touching, so it seems,
icons of verisimilitude.

Of this the dampness is not certain.
Nothing stops
until the hopes of falsity

fortuitously
drop from the trees
that are protecting this house.

So I divide myself into geographies;
old highways rot.
Farms become freeways
and cities sprout from my genitals.

Anything scrubs the immaculate
noose that life makes,
dangerous with flies,
touches the opening (soggy)
that encloses the room of doorways
that encloses the shore
that is opening the door.

Her April Opened At The Sign
Of The White Pomade

Her April opened at the sign of the white pomade
and he felt the doorway coming toward him.
She turned, entered, and began to play the player piano.

But his blue snow autobiography was as far as I could go
and this was how they captured me, as it were,
completely embedded inside the daydream.
Threading needles. Was of huge exceptions
that in order to touch, rooms away, I folded.

From this, gauging more than was really necessary,
to the terrace we meandered, leaderless and brown,
unable to notice the traps that reached out for us.

Was within. On the radiator, they tested it.
Content with, their riches, the cushion, the kitchen.
For you don't realize what you have until you have it.
On the seat here is room for things made since,
watching their pinned moth, the lamp shadows made
an audience of that time, of that place.

World of celestial immigrants! Not by bread or blood.
For you wrote me a long letter on damask,
fingering my pocket through the sentence structure.
That itself even entails this rapture or nails it.

That hand stammering, cataleptical, sprouts
for you, voice lingering. Door, bang.
The stroll made flexible became a screw.
Was that he secured so secretly.

The square root towards the masturbation in proportion,
of harmony, bound, this existence reeks
and houses garden, of foxglove shimmering through
hot wind that seeks the prosperities of sexless.

The shrubbery also. The penis, the cock. The disorder.
Through deserted cracks, the rope with manners.
Through mustard greens, I idle in this society.
I do my nothing before the man; on my table.

And many were the hands of my dream, bright blue,
through which some people, throughtful, dressed.
Expeditions before, were of glass. To balance softly
countries of psychology that work so generously.

Ship

Something too glossy
under the tent
repeats the phraseology.

Poor stone! And
ready or not, melting,
I come up for air,
shivering.

Emptying the glass,
I have visions of oddness
and of sweetness.

For each and every morning I am
towed by the tug
down through islands
of etymology
where cameras
navigate the kill.

And even the crowds that
amble towards these monuments
can't help
hearing the thud.

So why do these wave-lengths
harbor psychology,
ending in their spectrum
natatoriums?

Together, nude from the waist, we
open the window
to hear with our skin
how the ocean
empties itself,

solving the puzzle of
misused underwear and
natatorium.

I banish the climate,
notwithstanding.

For each and every summer the same thing
enters the cave, eats,
vanishes,
ending the cloud.

Why do you pay me?
How is it that
I fall asleep so easily?

Can anyone be thanked?

O window of the landscape
wide open and
totally
hollow to the touch
and totally
target-proof
that somehow
helps me
enter the ocean's
ocean!

Come lean with me
endlessly over
anthills,
nude in front of the
houselights.

For now is the time
I cannot hold
so heavenly crushed by
each
dry omen of touch.

I disintegrate again.

Perhaps the steamship will vanish

entirely
now that the ocean has vanished.

For no one can know the
gunboats that
often, childishly,
forget their ranchhands.

Altruism comes and goes,
narcissistically.

I vanish.

And when the daylight
hands me
each small particle of
negation,

I shift my angle,
touch my toes and
slowly sink into the
railroad station.

The Lights

These tall things don't need weeding.
But I can't get over the fireplace.
It's useless.
Except as an ashtray.

The lights stay on
and the windows remain wide open

I am standing outside of us
in another building
or in the other room.

I am safely lodged inside the
vulnerable.
I am the music of the traffic outside
and I am your complete body.

These states are unfallen
and into the ash
a window sticks its hand
to try out pieces of glass
the way a model
tries on style.

These stars too

and into the climate
winter burns a hole in the side of a hill.

The lights stay on
but the room fades out.

This is not noticed until later,
when the room returns,
harder,
more real than even the reality
of novels and films.

I drive my submission
like a beautiful icepick
into the bedspread of your life.

Poem

No one is drowning in the beautiful lake.

The Headlights

Slowly. And the fastness, interminable
with eyes closed
headlong into the headlight,
a sommersault into the moose.

A puddle opens up
through the oblong face.

It was a novel full of red hallways
and elevator shafts
and the way it ended
was not a great deal different

than the way it began.
She said. She said she would
retire into her feathery orchard,
Feeling his knee
pressed up against her abdomen.

And when they arrived and got out of
the long black car
the landscape was motionless.
A head appeared on the horizon,

a large blue whale
or a gas tank.

It began with a moose
in a long black car
and the head on the thin lip
of the horizon
spoke the word: Snow.

The wig itched. The hand
in the jacket
fingered a key

to the back door of an apartment
somewhere west
of what was then
considered respectable.

O whiteness!

It began with a plunge
into the terrors, the
skill, the bottom of the
sink.

She flew up and dissolved.
She became a gird.
She became a large flower.

It was a novel that
        couldn't be finished
and a harbor with doors.

It was a Lincoln Continental
        that they rode in
jammed together in the back seat.

After the seascape,
the land,
and after the landscape,
the face.

It was a novel full of beginnings
and endings
and the way it was ended
was the way it began:

She became a large flower,
a flame.
She became "The Whiteness."

If only I were all the streetlights in any given town.

Memorandum

Remembering everything...But
I can't (I don't)
I'd rather forget those
beautiful apricot sunsets,
those lusty verandas,
those innumerable flagpoles
placed at random.

*   *   *

I must try to remember
all of these things.
I can hardly forget.
Time passes. A freight train.

*   *   *

So I would rather forget
your aluminum smile.
I'd rather forget your
jalopy roadster
smoldering cozily
on the bank of the road

*   *   *

Note: please remember
to take out the garbage
and to take out the dog
and to take out your teeth.

*   *   *

I remember it!
I was reading a book
when suddenly the door
behind me opened.
In you walked with your tail

between your legs
and you talked about
my new white cloud.

*   *   *

Why were you crying?

*   *   *

A stick in the woods
turns into a snake.
The snake begins eating itself.

*   *   *

I am walking in a bathing suit
down a soft tar road
looking for berries
or wet magazines.

*   *

O I wish I could remember the name
of your pet dog "Henry."
You had named him after
your dead brother
who was also named "Henry."

*   *   *   *

I wish I could remember
the way you looked,
dressed in your gingham
housedress, playing "Mother"
as you stood on the back porch
like Lizzie Borden,
calling loudly through the rain,
"Henry! Henry! It's raining!"

* * *

I wish I could forget
that I am always remembering
what I want to forget.

* * *

I wish I could remember
what you were wearing yesterday,
then I would be able to remember
exactly which of your blue dresses
I spilled my paint box on

* * *

Or the way you enter a room
hesitantly,
or the way you leave a room
violently.

* * *

I wish I could remember
the rules of your
game called "Mother,"
then I would be able to remember
the rules of my game
called "Father."

* * *

But this train keeps on going
like a smooth snake
on the surface of the water,
revealing itself.

* * *

I am somewhere in the caboose
smoking my pipe
as we pass through Oklahoma
as we pass through Atlantic City.

* * *

I am dreaming about a long book
about a village
on the outskirts of your face,
about a mole on the lower
part of your back,
and about my snake tattoo.

* * *

What brand of cigarettes
do you smoke?

* * *

I remember the elephant tattoo
with the fly on it
and the ribbons
that your brother had
on his instep
and the elaborate heart tattoo
between his tiny shoulder-blades.

* * *

I remember the tattooed lady
in the circus sideshow(ca. 1942).
I have a photograph of her
———50¢.

* * *

I remember the sailor who
had bluebirds on his behind and

the other one
who had bluebirds
pecking at the nipples of
his completely hairless chest.

*   *   *

I remember now that I don't
have any tattoos at all.

*   *   *

I remember the circus when it came
and the man who whipped
his wife with a bullwhip
that was like a very long snake
and he whipped cigarettes
right out of her mouth.

*   *   *

What brand do you smoke?

*   *   *

I remember the "swami"
who went into a trance
and climbed a ladder
of swords.

*   *   *

I am climbing
that ladder of swords.

*   *   *

I am a train with orange lips
and a baggage car
full of elephants and
tattoo apparatus.

* * *

I am a train traveling
between a mountain and a river
moving up a hill.

* * *

So please remember
that I am a train
and not a bus.

* * *

Remember that the rain
that always annoys you so much
is good for the plants
and the trees.

* * *

Please remember my face
as my face is now
because in just a short while
this face, pressed up against
the window of the train
that races past you
will as I finish this sentence
no longer be this face.

* * *

Try to remember
sailboats, raincoats,
school nurses wearing white shoes.

* * *

Try to remember
the combination to

the safe deposit box
that contains
all kinds of treasure maps.

                    *   *   *

Have you ever had
something "on the tip
of your tongue?"

                    *   *   *

Try to remember
the tip of your tongue.

                    *   *   *

...I think this train is making
a circle.
Deja vu.

                    *   *   *

Or is it a spiral?

                    *   *   *

Is this train winding
up the mountain
or is it winding down?

                    *   *   *

O now I remember everything
as clear as day
now that I am the engineer
of this beautiful train.

                    *   *   *

I see myself at a window
above a train station.
Behind me
through the other window
are the sailboats
and below me
there is a train accident.

*   *   *

Remember this train accident.

*   *   *

Remember (if you can)
the color of my eyes.
Remember my eyebrows.

*   *   *

Remember (if you can)
that you never really
knew me.

*   *   *

Deja vu

*   *   *

"Have you ever been to
Atlantic City?" someone asks,
and I try to stop my answer
but my substitute answer
turns out to be
the same answer I gave
when I was here before.

*   *   *

We enter the Pullman car
in our bathing suits
and the Pullman becomes
a hallway of flags.

* * *

At the end of the hallway
is the beginning
of your story about
that rainy night in Atlantic
                                    City,
eating socks.

* * *

I am a train with bushy eyebrows
and a naked brakeman
 who moans:
"Again we are passing
the outskirts of Atlantic City!"

* * *

The engine of this train
is in love with the caboose
of this train.

* * *

The engine swallows the caboose
and then the baggage car
and then the Pullman
and the dining cars
and the passenger cars
and the engine.

* * *

O I wish I could remember
the right words to say

when I am entering
your apartment house.

*   *   *

I wish I could remember
the floor, the room, the zone.
I wish I could remember
your name
or the name of your dead brother.

*   *   *

O I wish I could remember
the first time I met you
and the way you stood there
holding a bunch of flowers,
on March 18th, 1957, 8 PM,
on the railroad platform.

*   *   *

I wish I could remember
my childhood
or the way this poem began.

*   *   *

For who would have expected
that someone like myself
could grow old and die
without some kind of terrible
accident
or without some kind of childhood?

*   *   *

I wish I could remember
what it was
that I have always
wanted so much to forget.

*   *   *

You Never Know What's Going to Happen Next

You never know what's going to happen next.

The Metaphysical Paintings

1. *The Enigma of Arrival*

We are nude beneath our costumes
as in the false myths we have been forced
to memorize
and there is a mistake in your eyes.

We are not aware that at last
the last offical has arrived,

Since the sky is false
I tell you falsely of my absence of feelings.

And you stand there staring down
counting the toes
that peek from out beneath
the hem of your theatrical robe.

2. *The Melancholy of an Afternoon*

The two of us make love
in the form of identical vegetables,
in shade,
oblivious to noise
and vanishing parades,
oblivious to flags
or that which tries to harm us
from the top of the industrial tower.

3. *A Grand Tour*

A mistake. It is a tower and not a tour
that does not crumble.
And we will make arrangements now
to take a guided tour of this tower

and soon find out that there are no stairs
and when you get to the top
there is no view.

4. *Departure of a Friend*

I see you lying on a candy-striped towel
face-down
reading a book of small pictures,
a book about Michelangelo

Goodbye.

But the time is wrong.
we discover that the train has already left.

It is a false goodbye.
Our shadows become one long shadow
that touches a pool.

Why is it that the railroad station is at times
so quiet? So empty?

5. *Nostalgia for the Infinite*

I will miss your loose-leaf notebooks
and your figs.
I will miss your calculated mistakes
and the pictures you sometimes liked to take.

We are still saying goodbye.
Same time. Same light. Same railroad
station.

Are you about to enter this different tower?
Are you about to become another?
A railroad engineer or a policeman?

Are you about to vanish?

6. *Love.Song*

O how I have loved you,
O great and classical world,
the way a child loves his father;
but now the time has come
to escape your betrayal.

Only the geometry of a green sphere.
Only the surgery upon a puff of smoke
can save us from more primitive forms
of this industrial sadness!

7. *Mystery and Melancholy of a Street*

At that time of day when guardian angels
have retired for the day,
as a small girl with a hoop,
I am menaced by the shadow of a guardian angel.

My substance is of shadow.

I let this angel follow me into the bowels
of an empty moving van;
I am raped by the sun.

I take off my shoes.

I wipe the sweat from his brow
with the hem of my Communion dress.

8. *The Enigma of Fate*

One move of the invisible queen,
one shout from the top of the stack,
one hand for the future,
and the spilling of seed.

One road through the labyrinth,
one turn to the left,
and the spilling of seed.

9. *Melancholy of an Autumn Afternoon*

We are still saying goodbye.

10. *The Naval Barracks*

At an early age, I was expelled
from the Naval Academy.
How well I remember those long Euclidian walks
into the sunset
at the end of a geometrical day.

Accumulations! Neat debris!
The magic of an ammunition dump!

The false perspective of my souvenirs
returns to haunt me.

Patient arrangements of frustrations.
Private mottos.
Public demonstrations of the insatiable
and the obvious!

11. *Purity of a Dream*

The purity of my dream can only be maintained
at the expense of the present.

I make a billboard in celebration
of our new found spring.
All the buildings start walking up the highway
to look at it.
They crowd around.

Now that I have made this billboard,
I can carry your picture around in my brain
in a small green suitcase
as I fall asleep
on that small train puffing into the distance.

12. *Masks*

I like this room. I like this movie of myself.
This view of the antiseptic town.

You are my mask
and I am yours.

Empty!

13. *Hector and Andromache*

At last we are together. Our dreams like our shadows
have at last combined.
We observe the higher mathematics
of our consistent departure.

We interfuse.

The geometry of our inter-relationship
has become like the demolished city
and the preserved city——

a train station that arrows towards
a new release of political crime,
a vertical of deliverance.

Hunger

Lakes of surprising shape
anchor these hills to the road
that goes from here to there
and can't return to where
this vanity began.

And the field of gray weeds
dumps as it bleeds
archaeology upon
some worried but unguarded
handsome young travelers

Actual structure, however,
is emotional not mental

Likewise, wise old men
and their busy houseboats
never touch the stuff.

Loud stars make a brain pattern
aptly upon the firmament
nailing the dance to an old hat
and a dancer who is deaf. (!)

Should all these orchestras
be cognizant of pain
an orchestra would burn.

Sadness in itself is not sad enough
to mend the rent
and terror cannot render
pain or push or error
elegant enough to be mirrors
large enough to bend.

An arrow strikes the head of
narrow peripheries
damned by scope

silently to cheat the bargains
cheating has supplied.

An elevator fails to deliver
Philadelphia's fair-haired boy.
The elevator starts and stops
languidly in the sunset
and an anger takes a dive.

Nothing can be expected of this,
the damaged, the
"stoned."

Empty landscapes increase in size
lacking only wit,

the way in which
the animals lack a language
to negotiate their anxieties
down surrogate byways of the ornamental
proprieties
and storefronts, heavy with whips.

Can all these factories
ammend the exclusions?
Purify? Or brighten a shadow
edging along the highway?

Lovely elm trees corner the land
and mark the hidden places where
misplaced maps were buried
maybe twenty or thirty years ago.

Cars, those speeding beads upon
a necklace that divides
patience from its panoply,
eat each other majestically,
lacking only dreams to make them
ancestral or
Norwegian.

Nevertheless, the careless grass,
dyed by rain a deeper green,
smells nice.
Cool fruit in the shade
and paper napkins
end the ending of a nap.

And the piles of newsprint rot
each summer,
for lacking the train
another landscape
nudges the rainbarrel
and another voice calls hiddenly
for an activity not really required
but certainly necessary.

Softly the wind unwinds around
careless statuary
arranged in attitudes of finance,
perhaps too sensuously.

Local bombast beacons the finality
of an open bowl
not necessarily empty
but damp,
solely to hide the anger
cartons make,

adding this to that,
cartoon-like,
partitioning lakes.

Enough of too little. Too much of
length instead of largeness.
Apples, for instance,
nipped. Or grapes in a harbor
shining roundly
and exchanging the air.

Could all these outlets be
an inlet for some loss?
Poison for a shouting
insanely dreamed?

Lakes are skillfully arranged
by someone, perhaps yourself,
not in the usual fashion,
clock-wise,
but slowly against the weather,
carefully,
alphabetically by size.

Practical vandals knock the occasion,
each portion of the public
or the secretions of this garden,
as amateurs celebrate the public
in private
or as if these odors were a secret.

A loudness we have learned to like
softens the oddness
and the oddness breaks out
neatly into the open
surprising only the avenues that lead
to affluent drugstores.

Systematically, in even rows,
even the plantings that have refused to bloom
bloom
and establish a kind of foreign aid
that reduces the exposure.

Eels, clouds, guns
learn to lean on
an air that does not move.

Love's hate buys food for
animal pastures
and the disasters are not green

but hallucinatory
and faintly redundant
when they glow like ashtrays
in the middle of the dark.

Never again will this view
dump ashes on the lake,
so carelessly
causing the binoculars to grow
agrarian sores upon the fertility
of insubstantial, inexpensive reproductions
of a painting we have decided
never again to like.

1. Grand words crumble in the face of
actions taken arbitrarilly,
nudging grandeur off this road,
daring it to be real.

2. Summer's younger swimmers
continue to be brave
in spite of that which circles
high above the oval
pulled by the varieties
that each one needs.

3. Precisely.
For precisely at this moment
eating becomes a living.

4. Loaned out, butchered, fragmentized,
actual feelings are, so it seems,
not actual at all. But
don't mistake the actual for
something that is real,
for couldn't a language be a collection
of some infinite emotions
and not a definition of mere thought?

Leaves grow through a corpse
and the corpse gets up and walks,
nips a dog,
but doesn't return home
for home is so beautifully hidden
in this completely open place,
alive with tenderness.

Untitled

1.

I am the one, within or without, who
mentions your name in code in cold, unfriendly
places that are continued on some other page.

Open places, sliced by lawns,
singled out by handsome, toothless,
slightly balding, professional assassins.

I'm the partner. Or your bud. Your publicity.
But the followers learn to tax,
leaving these words behind you or else you'll
endanger our brand new civilization?

2.

Toenails are the delicate. Pine trees. Etc.
Hold over. The contents of this cardboard,
expereincing only what I am able to allow you too.

3.

Sunrise related to your most distant star
understands this retreat from sensory factors.
Nor will I attempt to approximate.
Sorry. You. And your kindness are

                         the available facilities
to touch or to resemble. So you
Sail away   Breathing. Heavily.

4.

    Largeness?   So am I. So how about some quick food or

another pastime? Your elderly?
    The.   It's sandwiches.
      Essential.   But.   We.   You know what I mean.
  Lousy connections.   Phoney food. The
you. Your ambitious sexuality. Your tobacco thing.

5.

Hurting you is hurting the worldliness
and it doesn't matter anymore whom I love
very seldomly. You're not the sun shining
every other morning anyway.   You're you.

6.

Buying up this choice real estate has been
entirely satisfactory to my new sense of ego-development.
Even if it doesn't make you feel guilty! Besides
no one has ever even ever been here once before.

1.

ı am the one.....................without............
mentions.................cold, unfriendly
places that are ....age.

Open....laces.....lice..... .....
single......out by hand.....tooth.......
slight.............profess..........ass......

I'm the part ....our.... ....city

But......low........ear..........
leaving......or.......behind................
endanger our brand ....

7.

1.) No one here is foolish enough to believe
   in these lies
      that wouldn't even fool your publicity.

2.) Another person enters the sidecar
      and is swept aside by your
         train of gadgets to behold in their entirety.

3.) The witnesses are reliable.

4.) Underwear is unnecessary. So's the weather
      we're exposed to by the elements.

5.) Ruined. We are ruined by the new star system.

6.) Entrance.

8.

I am the folding of the
slippery. What?

9.

Exclusive. Brand New Civilization, following up the
martyrdom............You dark. You dare to.
Buying up the star-funnels on a budget.
And as usual the business will continue
reluctantly for you are the last word of my novel,
resulting in push-ups. These. These hold-overs.

And further more,
sorry.
Sorry I am the one and only, the most.
I am the you lack. You struck,
nothing here and now the superiority and my

gathering up of all these telephone directories.

10.

I am you are of your
nothingness. You ploy.

11.

May I mention that to all those here
you are among the least flavored?

12.

Delivering the barge breast-plate.   It's of aluminum, right?
as is the aluminum.   And also the barge.
You too are of aluminum,   You aluminum vendor.

13.

I am the vision. Slump.

5.

"Hurting you is hurting the worldliness
and it doesn't matter anymore whom I love
very seldomly. You're not the sun shining
every other morning anyway.   You're you."

14.

Sincerity————mine, yours, theirs————has been blemished
electrically by the........ toenail.

Elaboration becomes too simple by this time.
Now is the time for less elaboration! More fun!

15.

Better behave yourself under these mutual circumstances.
Even the evening can go wrong and end up

taking too much or falling off the edge.

Even the sky can pull a false curtain,
remembering the morality that is used as a cushion.

16.

Ladders fall from the sky. The sky. We
operate on a shoestring
of your savings   account passbook, once lost.
Kindly   The we.   My house.
I found them, inside.

                    Greatness falls apart.

17.

Capable stagehands map out the supposed pathway
adjacent to the retrieved from the fresh.
Lost. Finding rooming houses conducive.
Nap time. Canada. His mouth claims alms and then
descends the iron stairway to the chauffeur's.

And tongues keep clomping the chump who is
reasonably salacious, insistently so, or
sufficiently morose to have inspired the April.

18.

Winter turns your furnace on and
  how I love these poses so repeatedly stomped,
   you following everywhere I don't...

8.

   I am the folding of the
   slippery. What?

19.

The financial arrangements were interminable.
Railroads, etc. But your arm over my chair
understood the dimensions of the spectacular
the redundant manifestations of the
horrible, your blunderous tree

20.

and then she glided succinctly into the far corner,
loafed a bit
   in the manner she was accustomed to,
while her partner,
    the gross,
     the bending,
approached a new way of reading.

You pinched her nose and then
said that you are leaving for   *Canada.*

21.

Sorry to have replaced the unfortunate.
Oh.

22.

Our cruel September when the heat's been on inside
basement storehouses! He'll unbutton the pretender.

Victory must at last be near. I hope.
I continue to believe in your soft spots

of your sadly
under the cool chair
shade and all the other combustibles.

23.

Although there were once blunt lawns to cut
nothing now is withstanding the onslaught of your
deliciousness..................................

24.

Until this very movement there were lots of things to
negate with the edges
but now there are only pages to count and
embellishments

Lap that mentions a groove for the daytime.
I come with my forehead.

Embrocations instead of evocations or vacationlands
vying for the tax,
angelic tax
bubble in the homestead of your harrassed bunk.

Larger than life and smaller than death,
epicurean try-outs of the brand new civilization!

13.

I am the wisdom........Slurp, slurp.

25.

Spirals bandage up the vanquished
plot concerning the overthrow.
Enemy camels fall feet first into the clump,
nabob talc: your breezeway. Goat's milk. To
damn these incalculable blood-suckers!

11.

(May I mention that to all those here
you are among the least flavored?)

26.

Apex meat collossus! Juniper berry
forever hounding: She valued the

thatness of her shadow stretched
entertainingly through several bygones,
resulting in a damaged.

Begging the inconclusiveness of the daylight
our majestrate was the pubescense of
original sunning. Those blisters then were
not the subsistance of the wink.

10.

(I am you are of   your

128

nothingness. You   ploy.)

27.

Barbarian seacoasts cost more when purchased slowly
and at arm's length. To deny this is
redundant   You
burn.   I am the caucus inside the delicious
equatorial: You. And.
Redundant time-cycle of the Northerly returns.

28.

Stalemate heaven.
Hopscotch butterscotch.
Opener.
Principle cities
Stalemate.

29.

Which one is the foremost in these quarters?
Are you sure that you will be able to return when
      the returns come in, in order to invalidate the
      requirements?
In what way are you the most flavored?
To open it, what is required? Is it really necessary
      to utilize the electricity?
In twenty-five words or less, will you explain your
      reasons for disappearing? Was it because of the
      train schedule?
Now are you ready to begin all over again?
Gaining? What are you about to loose when
      the new month begins with a flush?

11.

May I mention to all those here
you are among the least flavored?

30.

Tigerama / Ghost town / Rama / Madness
Underwear / Dash / Resultant / Whispers
Rodeo / Cyclone / Captain Video / Dapper
Naptha / Leap / Tonto / Cherry-vanilla

31.

Roadwise, you are resplendant in your brand new rags
equivalent to the people who are restlessness.
Again tonight. Again tonight. Again tonight.

Dining out. I like the cut of your blouse. The color.
I like the way you put your arm on the back of my chariot

Not now. Please not now. I need to rest a bit and then.
go out for a wilt without your forlornliness.

32.

AND THEN SHE GLIDED SUCCINTLY INTO THE FAR CORNER
LOAFED A BIT IN THE MANNER SHE WAS ACCUSTOMED TO,
LUNGED AND THEN LIFTED THE SMALL CURTAINS.

2.

Toenails are the delicate. Pine trees. Etc.
Hold over. The contents of this cardboard,
experiencing only what I am able to allow you too.

33.

Suggestions from the floor are welcome in spite of
my failure to recognize the table.

"And then when it came to be the new era
life expanded all over the place in direct proportion to
loveliness of the way you kissed my forehead."

34.

Afterwards, the pine trees.

Delicately, the rent.

Sadly, the rest of them were arriving.

10.

I   am   the   are   of   your
nothingness.   You   play   .

35.

Adequacy in the face of the terminal becomes these
delicately scented
                          footnotes to a major work stoppage,
venturing out towards the assassinations,
          excercising the completeness that is multiple.

Noteworthies become homebodies
The down. The approximate bunk. finished off
under the table,

reassuring the rest of your tribal
                          that there are no
eternities more sophisticated.

36.

My poundage over on steerage replaces the muscle.
and you float up above the pine trees in your gladness,
ghosting the speeches I have not prepared which
accept everything about you without squirming.

Zonked by language.

I continue the toenails
needles of hay. The pronounced.
Entaglements untangle and I fall down
somehow into the morning, noon and night.

The Yellowing

I

I am afraid and
actually buy up
most of these
notions that are
old-fashioned

to eat them,
and quietly to
narrow down the
yellowing.

our dumb delight
now pleases
each microcosm
instead of
nose-dives or
perimeters
articulated by
ramps.

Touch these
increased potatoes,
carefully.
Undo this head.

Lately these
archways are
repeating
and finally
cause rivers to
hollow the stopped
engine of my
winter and my
intentional clue.

Now too these
glamorous
garden landmarks
undermine the
mouth wash folders,

warping the time
real time takes
and tither away
poorly, if alone, on
paper or mistakes.

Evil is as evil
remembers these
answers sometimes to be.

So I'll buy more
time, borne loosely,
roaming streets,
end the ending,
time the time,

liking only
islands of their
gay equivalents.

How can I stop
these tactics?

Some of them
touch your hand with
interior timespans,
landing near
luxuries that
show factories
or falsetto,
melodic,
engine flanks.

How can I banish
old stepping stones
without a defeat?

I and my
meal-ticket
and your
neighborhood rules
all fall down
greatly muffed by
equal language.

The missing
options multiply
exquisitely in
X-ray cubes:

I buy the
standard
torments
as if I
needed time to
develop tubes.

And then the
sundial moves.

Everyone who is
an old friend
caught in time or
habits of
desire has the
answers that are
yellowing or lean.

Somehow, however, I can't
touch bottom
and I can't
reach for
the top, either

So I'm stranded
in this puzzlement.

Movements are the
answers,
not yours but my
answers,

giving away the
entrance place,
the corporation
or the face,

leaving all my
evil ways
alone to die out
very slowly over many
evil days.

My many filters
yearn for brighter,
nicer, neater,
icicle days.

Can I be
evil if evil
warns?

And can I ever
return these
memory blanks?

Because I seem to
enter I am
downed by
friendly, but colorless,
equations and bad
examples of the light.

Later on the
instant pudding mix
necessitates
giving or
taking or
half-way positions.

Another reason is
this: my
purity when
engaging in
riffs.

Holding this I
approach the frozen
perhaps too
slowly or with

too many
old-fashioned
diatribes
against the
yellowing.

So I'll leave again
or try. I'll
move from here to
everywhere.

That settles that.

However,
it's formal and
not completely
gallant to
be, if being is this,
each day,
another logic
under the logic of
the everyday.

I'm basically foreign
for I'm not here
unless the
lukewarm melts.

Well, it won't.
It can't. It
lacks the brand new
licencing procedure,

holds it up by
another lump,
picks the
proper
entry and then
noses it out.

I pass
the vitality, the
neatness to the
English Language,
violence to the word.

Engineering problems
run up bills of
domesticity and
opera scores.

Excursions and
scores comply with

the failures of the
house that
is too large;
some sleep or
injure the
nationality.

I'm at the center of
this explosion that

silently, slowly
explodes.

Loneliness is
foreign. Loneliness
is so
soft it
booms. It's an
epidemic
and   full of bad
underwear.

Tenderness is,
if tender,
full of
upkeep and the
like.

Il

I am afraid and
actually buy up
most of these
notions that are
old-fashioned

to eat them
and quietly to
narrow down the
yellowing.

   Our dumb delight
now pleases
each microcosm
instead of
nose-dives or
perimeters
articulated by
ramps.

Touch these
increased potatoes,
carefully.
Undo this head.

Lately these
archways are
repeating the climactic

and finally
possible hoists
have their very own
ice coatings,
like it or not.

Our deliberate oracle,
sideways,
often elliptical,
perhaps this
harbinger
is not mysterious.

Cautiously, I
address the
loveliness with my
stand-offishness,
hop a plane
or just escape
again into the
stand-offishness.

How's that for
enemy groundwork,
evil with cause?

Time and time again
our plans
falter,
pushing out the
answers from their

pauses,
endangering
repeating
punishments that
evoke more crime.

Regional problems
halt all time
and broadcast
perceptual doubt
so that I find that

I am lying to you
again. I can't
move loosely.
Looseness is a shade of
yellowing
inside the bomb
not correctly timed.

Going, going,
almost gone.
Not here but
otherwise here.

Touching you,
how can I
empty out this
ripeness?

Our islands! I
need some
envelopes.

Our possible
futures,
mix these omens!

Your region is too
valuable to

enter
repeatedly.

Yellowing
bends the light
another way but the
dying is
habitual
as is the
biology.

Islands converge upon
this mythology,
sinking it.

I balance these
formalities upon
salient wellsprings,
ordering luck.

Aren't you ready yet
to forgive these
leanings
each clear movement
accumulates
so softly and so
toughly?

Never mind.

Our flight plans
orchestrate the
necessary signals,
entering my dream hut,
caused by
all your
naked bodies.

Beginning here
equal mountains

hurry
under the
rainstorm
towards

beautiful nights of
youth and tender
sadness.

Understanding this is
curiously hard,
hoping for
silence or for
land.

Instant pudding
gains today while
heavens stain
the slight margin,

dangerously
enclosed, that
causes
evil to
push these
thin remarks towards

inland bombsights
opening the world
not yet ready to be
so suddenly startled.

Somatolysis

A mild form of insomnia jumps up and down
and falls into the rain puddle
you have just barely missed.
And when your arm comes back
you don't even recognize it.
But you recognize your name.

Why then are there so many knots and transfusions,
so varied an array
of horseplay bi-products and confusions?
Why the obvious? And why the immense?

Dark horses, for instance, fall into ambush parties
completely dismayed
at the turbulance of the flight pattern.

And while I slide from my hammock,
you, my partner in this delicious masquerade,
confess unwillingly to a cloud formation
your innermost joy.

Perhaps as you stand there with your eyes half-closed
you don't really see that a bird just landed.

If the hand were already open, most likely
you wouldn't go in.

So you see,
if I were to clear up all these little puzzles
that are rigged
bigger than life
in semaphors and bread baskets
devoid of metaphors,

these cyphers and mistakes,
fooling only those
who take,
          as they say,
the icing for the cake,

then I (you) would be the allusion that's erased
inside the foreground of the sentence structure,

and you (me), whoever you are or whoever you may yet be,
would be left with a meaning
that has no
gesture of acceptance or of dreaming.

        A dream about false clues
        in the form of
        footprints leading backwards
        to a triangular lake;

        a dream about open highways
        strewn with teaspoons
        made of green glass;

        a dream about a dream
        in which a vanilla propeller
        breaks loose.

So all these jigsaw puzzles shaped like shape itself
or shaped like landscape crossword puzzles
missing one key piece
or shaped like cloud hangovers
or the shapelessness of fleece

cannot be replaced by translations
or transitions into the objects of this place
but are replaced by enigmas more numerous
more arcane
than the surface or the odors they name.

You are about to tell me something very important
but characteristically
you forget what it is
and spend, I might add,
the rest of the afternoon trying to remember.

You (I) fall asleep on the sailboat
and the sailboat sails out to sea
and when you awaken there is no one around.

I, however, am safely ashore
basing my calculation on the permutations
of several contradictory
theories of motivation and sense perception.

At this point then in this flatland,
sufficiently linguistically removed,
we could very easily find ourselves fond of
the particulars as opposed to
the abstractions,
those perpendiculars of necessity
that we are supposed to
uphold and rejoice in.

But famous rose breeders are discovered
on the outskirts of the farm
bleeding to death
in neat rows of bicycle debris
as the heat increases over this place
promising once again,
                              for the third time this week,
more rain.

Further west, on the eastern shore,
a vague listlessness of vegetable products
could, if I allowed it,
overwhelm the thickness of the consistency.

(Who are you? What are you doing
over there in the background?
Why are you hiding?)

Oh, yes. I forgot to tell you...
later on in the month I came upon the house
you so often talked about
and devised a message unit

that although, it can be read as real language
when held up to a mirror and decoded contains
sentences of contradictory meaning.

"Inveterate myopia is contagious
if you allow it to advance
beyond the preliminary stages
in which vanishing points become so prevalent
that they make the viewpoint resplendant
with small dark periods."

"Bewilderment is a symptom of self-abuse
as are all these floral 'raincoats'
that have been manipulated so dangerously
by your great-grandmother
who is well-known in these parts."

"Beware of the signpost and the awkwardness,
too carefully contrived,
of a signature that reeks of garlic
and then when held up to the heat
becomes an adjective instead of a noun."

Thusly, or at least theoretically,
we are free to make up the word games,
to describe the emotions
that because of their colors
(dots and stripes)
are able to melt into the dots and stripes
of the background field
that acts as a shield
composed of sounds and extengencies,

protecting the somnambulist from the sound of
pale green ambulances
or damp wind around the earlobes of,
let us say,
any given relativity of sore points
or grammatical, syntactical, ontological
inconsistencies of weight
or discrepencies of sight.

This then is a method of consciousness
or unconsciousness
as is reading into
and/or writing around
and filling in
the spaces surrounding
a few choice specimens of vocabulary:

The wall-eyed rag-pickers of Vera Cruz
find in their travel
specimens of pandamonium
which placed them in a jeep
where safe-crackers publish them in lieu
of the basic vocabulary
that is glorious with the bi-lateral.

I discover the wall-eyed in a small field
outside the Vera Cruz Hotel.
In the Pandamonium Room
I jeep the unfortunates with my crackers
that make these basic tactics
glorious with the tents of disease
and the organs of the bi-lateral.

or
What is glorious is also basic
but necessarily bi-lateral
or at least not as bi-lateral as you,
you with your wall-eyed makeshift,
you with your Vera Cruz crackers,
you with your pandamonium
and your well-oiled, well-heeled jeep.

or
Bi-lateral spaceships in their glorious
their basic, their crackers of room,
rid the jeep of its pandamonium
here in Vera Cruz, wall-eyed,
waiting for the truth.

or

Wall-eyed vocabulary,
pandamonium vocabulary,
jeep vocabulary
cracker vocabulary,
basic vocabulary,
glorious vocabulary,
bi-lateral vocabulary.

or

At last we have discovered the wall-eyed
inhabitants of the Great Wall of Vera Cruz
I take out my Pandamonium
and nail them to the bullet-proof jeep.
We eat the retrieved crackers
and the crackers made of enlargements.
These facts are basic.
Thusly, in our search for the glorious
we become bilateral.
We become as small children
or large birds
enamored of the brilliantly shiny.

You— —or is it really me
in still yet another of my
terrific disguises?———
will lift the seedpod
and deposit the gum
carefully and with great skill
beneath the canvas landscape
so artfully stretched
upon a wooden support
shaped like a bread basket.

Shaped like a piece from a jigsaw puzzle
made from a mirror,
you will caress the trigger and shoot the gun
that has been following you
like a small white sun

in and out of unnecessary stanzas
and terrific cadenzas,
neat paragraphs of delay.

And then the beginning of the wind-swept day
I or you (who it is
doesn't really matter)

will remove the wrapper
from a package that has come in the mail
but only to discover
that the package is empty.

("You, whoever you are, are always playing
these tricks on me,
fooling my plan
with surprise messages or a word in only one hand
of the two hands you so often hide
behind your back
in the shadows of radios
or color TV sets disguised
as fishing nets or peculiar jewelry.")

And then when all these particles of compliancy
in pauses of film
are quiet enough to be visible,
I soothe. I soothe.
I somehow arrive at the airline terminal,
deplane,
and inside a telephone booth
expose the miraculous.

As if the miraculous could be exposed
or needed to be!

A dream of lodgings
incredibly narrow
with beds like 2 X 4's
——in a familiar foreign city,
in a clarity of absurd numbers;

a dream about cool water
and a gardner
with several mustaches;

a dream about meeting the Pope
who turns out to be
a great-grandmother in a housecoat.

We manage. We manage to keep
these headlines above water
so that everything is important
————from the slightest twitch
to the biggest explosion————
so that nothing seems to matter
or to exist
in any real sense
except in the sense of
that which our imaginations cannot get ahold of.

The package, however, was *not* really empty.

It contained anything we needed it to hold
or anything, no matter how unseemly
————your sock, my tongue————
we imagined it to contain.

Emptiness, therefore, is usefull,
as are these words,
in a sense,
so useful for meaning or protection
or bait.

These annoying surges, for instance,
that come from nowhere
and lift me (you) up so voluptuosly
or the urges that turn my head
with an insatiable, sweet-sad burning
then burn my hands with the distance of distance
and the closeness
as if I myself am merely this distance
or the closeness,

as if I am you
beneath these words
and you are me
as we melt into the background sounds,
undifferentiated, hidden,
ready to pounce.

You are, or so it would seem,
the inside meaning of the outside,
completely visible in these rudiments of style,
this codebook of key phrases.

Your sailboat sails out to sea
and because you do not remember
how to steer it
you can't come back again
until the wind turns around.

I, however, manage to swim.
I manage to get from here to there
without much effort,
avoiding the stem.

It's nice. And the warm bed of this
cool language
once-removed from the necessities of discourse
is a relief well-worth having,
a game of hide and seek
that elates
the way pure dabs of color,
describing nothing but themselves,
relieve the eyes and tease them
into new approximations of the invisible.

                              A dream of blue onions
                              winning the uphill race
                              instead of the bottles
                              that were supposed to;

a dream of sheer underwear
in a test to determine
short-sightedness
as opposed to non-tactility;

a dream of mortgages held
on obscure barnyards
covered at this moment
with a delicate wool fuzz.

So that old neighborhood of your convictions
complete with catch-phrases
held laboriously in the face of disaster,
dividing the world
into the focused and the blurred,
is almost gone,

casting a long shadow into the swimming pool
across the lawn
perhaps today for the last time.

It, the something, takes hold and fills your life
with the terror of poetry,
making little neat holes
approximately one inch in diameter
at random
through the oatmeal lists,
never touching the outline,

determining,
in its own veiled way,
what it is the outline does.

This duplicity falls into the omnipresent messiness
of imaginary handshakes
with a loud ouch
and a moan that shakes off sleepiness
in numerous ways,
incalculable,
and in incurable sentence fragments.

The vanishing points amidst the floral 'raincoats'
become signposts almost of the mirror
buried in an armchair covered with leaves.

(Who are you? Is that you again?
Why don't you ever come out of hiding?
Don't I know you from someplace else?)

But it is this language itself
that is so dangerous,
adding as it does
an emphasis that is invisible
under ordinary circumstances,
concealing the full weight of the expression.

Expression?

Words, after all, are a usefull disguise
made up of overlapping references
and deliberate lies.

But a disguise might also be philosophical
or metaphysical,
concealing beneath subordinate clauses
and a multiplicity of causes
resplendant with jargon
a simple honesty
or a need to be appreciated for small things
rather than for large systems.

You are no longer so to speak
"spiritually wall-eyed,"
but you are still a little deaf.
It's the wind and it's the sailboat
you have named after a word in this poem,
calling it "The Vera Cruz."

And, in spite of all the verbal pyrotechnics
and semantic pandamonium,
I think you are glad you found the jeep
hidden inside the hay-stack

and the fire-crackers
that when used
reveal a design in seven basic colors
that are glorious with significance
and not in the least bit "bi-lateral."

Another one of my ploys
becomes in this manner,
a species unaparalleled,
very discreet,
of white noise
full of bad breath, bad faith
and habits of exactitude
that cover up an opposite attitude.

Such slight activities———coding and decoding———
are harmless
even in spite of the fact
that the guns are all loaded
and we can do nothing but act

> A dream in the shape
> of a jigsaw puzzle piece
> that is like a place
> or an amoeba;
> a dream in the shape
> of a sailboat or a gun
> or a floral raincoat;
>
> a dream in the shape
> of a mask that looks like
> the face of the person behind it.

For I am lying in wait for you,
you the unsuspecting but curious bystander,
waiting for you to make the first move
in perhaps a series of moves,
not all of them pre-determined,
and to pass by where I wait
cleverly submerged into the pattern of the foliage,
into the pattern of words.

NEW POEMS

Poem (The Feebleness)

The   FEEBLENESS   only   ITSELF (You) IS   way
    She   (have)   *removed*
A DISEASE   to correct *..the* (only)   OF   these
    errors   THE   is to   *outer*
RECTUM. erase *covering,* HER AIM (yourself) them
and start (to) WAS   all over   (blame.)
  (I have)   again   (me) *revealing* on
OFF. *more*   (I have)   *sludge,*   SHE GOT (you.)
    a clean   *that*   sheet   *tasted*
  like   IT OFF   of HER paper.
  (I have)   (all these) *vanilla.*
CHEST. (spaces)   BI-PARTISAN   (to)
  Snow *Her* HORSEPLAY falls *penis* CATCHES UP
  in the middle (play *was*   of the
WITH   night   *enormous*   THE   CRUEL
and when with) JOKE   I awake (I play) *and* the countryside
HE   has been (with) PLAYED ON (myself.)
  as   erased. *big*   I can   *as*
hardly (It's) HER   (a game)
   WHEN *a baseball* recognize (you) THEY *bat.* WERE
(can't) TOGETHER *She* (possibly)   *kept*
  it   the landscape   which .was .*in*
    AT THE   once (understand.) BEACH.   (The)
(first) *a violin* (rule)   *case* so *and*
 familiar   THE   to me, (concerns TIDE
  CAME *only* as (the) IN. WHOLLY *removed* familiar
as (rectum.) IMAGINARY *it* the (Never) *on* (put)
sunny   back (anything) *days.* SEA CAPTAINS of
LECTURED (in) my   (it) *She*   THEM
(that) *would* ABOUT THEIR (is) *force* BAD *him* (larger)
  BEHAVIOR.   (than) (a telephone)   hand.
to   (booth) *lick* SHE *it.*   SANK.

Poem (To Smoke)

TO SMOKE   We were   THE DISTANCE   going away
INTO TWO   for (Some)   a long time.   SEPARATE
We packed   PARKS OR TWO   (times)   our bags   (I feel)
and said   (as if I am going to)   goodbye
FOLLOW THE (fall)   to our   BANNISTER friends
the dogs. (apart)   (at the seams)
(and)   REQUIRES   They (just)   FORTITUDE
OF A GREAT (be) cried. We   MAGNITUDE   (separated)
cried.   (into)   No use crying (what)
AND ALSO   over   SEVERAL
spilled (I)   DELIBERATE (was.)   BOAT RIDES.   milk.

Protest Poem

Death, unnatural   WE TRIED   (To) death is
OUR BEST (forget)   TO LOOK   (her)   on my   THE OTHER
    (problems)   mind and I am   WAY. WE   (and) reminded of
TRIED it every   TO CONTINUE   time I (the) MAKING POETRY
    (world) turn on   AND ART (problems) my television
THAT WOULD (she) set or CELEBRATE LIFE   (went)   read a
    BUT THE   newspaper. This   WORDS (on) war is   WERE
HOLLOW,   (a)   WORDS LIKE (shopping) a disgrace,
       JOY OR   a hoax, a device   PEACE OR   (spree.)
for keeping BEAUTY. OTHER WORDS (she) KEEP INTRUDING.
    (bought)   the American economy   WORDS LIKE (a new)
from collapsing   NAPALM OR   or changing   CREDIBILITY GAP.
   into something   SOME TRIED   (dress,)   more just.   TO PAINT
PICTURES OF No affluence   CHILDREN (a girdle)
        can justify   BUT THE (that)   these senseless
deaths, this   CHILDREN BECAME (was) torture, rape   CORPSES
EATEN   AWAY BY (cleverly) and injustice. (engineered)
There is NAPALM.SOME   blood on   TRIED TO (to) the American
  MAKE PAINTINGS (hide) THAT CELEBRATED   flag. There
(extra) HARMONY AND   (inches) is blood   NOBILITY BUT (of)
on every THE PAINTINGS (fat) WERE SPLATTERED American dollar
(and)   I am (she)   a poet   WITH INNOCENT (bought) and not
   (a) businessman. I am ashamed   I WEAR (new) of MY VIETNAM
country (color) SHOES. (television)   I EAT MY VIETNAM PIE.
SOLDIERS AND CIVILIANS The American ON Revolution (set.) has
become   ON BOTH SIDES   (She was able)   a dirty (to see) joke.
   (the war)   DIE   (in color.)   HORRIBLE DEATHS.

Seven Poems

I: *The Varieties*
    These repeats repeat
    the varieties of sleep
    in a glass house
    floating towards
    a drop in temperature,
    the edge of a cliff.

II: *Valley*
    These repeats repeat
    the varieties of sleep
    in a glass house
    floating towards
    a drop in temperature,
    the edge of a cliff.

III: *Cautious Clockwork*
    These repeats repeat
    the varieties of sleep
    in a glass house
    floating towards
    a drop in temperature,
    the edge of a cliff.

IV: *A Drop*
    These repeats repeat
    the varieties of sleep
    in a glass house
    floating towards
    a drop in temperature,
    the edge of a cliff.

V: *Dreams*
    These repeats repeat
    the varieties of sleep
    in a glass house
    floating towards
    a drop in temperature,
    the edge of a cliff.

VI: *Fire*
These repeats repeat
the varieties of sleep
in a glass house
floating towards
a drop in temperature,
the edge of a cliff.

VII: *The Edge of A Lake*
These repeats repeat
the varieties of sleep
in a glass house
floating towards
a drop in temperature,
the edge of a cliff.

Sonnet

all(10),almost(69),alone(11),and(6),and(16),and(24),
and(28),and(53),and(76),arising(88),art(52),at(84),
at(94),beweep(12),bootless(22),break(85),brings(104),
change(110),contented(62),cries(23),curse(29),day(87),
deaf(18),desiring(49),despising(70),disgrace(3),earth
(91),enjoy(61),eyes(8),fate(31),featured(41),for(97),
fortune(5),friends(47),from(89),gate(96),haply(71),
heaven(19),heaven's(95),him(43),him(45),hope(40),
hymns(93),I(9),I(59),I(72),I(107),in(2),in(39),in(65)
kings(114),lark(83),least(63),like(34),like(42),like
(44),like(80),look(25),love(100),man's(51),man's(55),
me(33),men's(7),more(37),most(60),my(13),my(21),my(30),
my(78),my(111),myself(27),myself(68),of(86),on(74),
one(36),outcast(14),possest(48),remembered(101),rich
(38),scope(56),scorn(108),sings(92),state(15),state
(79),state(112),such(102),sullen(90),sweet(99),that
(54),that(105),the(82),thee(75),then(77),then(106),
these(66),think(73),this(50),thy(98),to(35),to(109),
trouble(17),upon(26),wealth(103),what(58),when(1),
wishing(32),with(4),with(20),with(46),with(57),with
(113),yet(64).

Questionnaire

1. My age is: (A) 1-19, (B) 20-21, (C) 22-25, (D) 26-29, (E) *30-33*, (F) 34-38, (G) 39-44.

2. My height is: (A) Under 5', (B) 5' to 5'2", (C) 5'3" to 5'5", (D) 5'6" to 5'8", (E) *5'9" to 5'11"*, (F) 6' to 6'2", (G) 6'3" to 6'5", (H) 6'6" or over.

3. I am: (A) Slight framed, (B) *Medium framed*, (C) Large framed.

4. My education level is: (A) High school graduate, (B) Vocational school graduate, (C) 1 year of college, (D) 2 years of college, (E) *3 years of college*, (F) College graduate, (G) Masters Degree, (H) Ph.D. degree, (I) Other post-graduate or professional degree.

5. My hair color is: (A) Blonde, (B) Red, (C) *Brown*, (D) Black.

6. I am fluent in: (A) Spanish, (B) German, (C) French, (D) Italian, (E) Yiddish, (F) Chinese, (G) Russian, (H) *none*.

7. My race is: (A) *Caucasian*, (B) Negro, (C) Oriental.

8. My religion is: (A) Protestant, (B) Catholic, (C) Jewish, (D) Agnostic, (E) atheist, (F) *Unaffiliated deist*, (G) Irrelevant.

9. My political convictions are: (A) Middle of the road, (B) *Left of center*, (C) Right of center, (D) Irrelevant.

10. I: (A) *Have never been married*, (B) Am divorced, no children, (C) Am widowed, no children, (D) Am divorced, with children, (E) Am widowed, with children.

11. Most people consider me: (A) *Introverted*, (B) Extroverted, (C) in between.

12. How many brothers and sisters do you have? (A) None, (B) 1, (C) *2*, (D) 3, (E) 4, (F) 5, (G) 6 or more.

13. I drink alcoholic beverages other than beer or wine): (A) *Socially*, (B) Occasionally (a drink or two a week or less), (C) Never.

14. It is important to achieve: (A) Social Status, (B) Financial security, (C) Wealth, (D) *Inner Peace*.

*   *   *

15. It's who you know that counts, rather than what you know. *False*.

16. If my steak does not come out the way I ordered it, I will not ask the waiter to take it back. *False*.

17. I am a "take charge" kind of person. *False*.

18. If other factors seem to be working out, sex is not important in marriage. *False*.

19. How much money you earn is more important than the kind of work you do. *False*.

20. I often get involved in a friend's problems. *True*.

21. It's embarrassing to be the first one out on the dance floor. *False*.

22. It's great to have a day with absolutely nothing to do. *True*.

23. It's better to have a few close friends than a great many acquintances. *True*.

24. When something new comes along I am one of the first to try it. *True*.

25. I prefer big active parties to small, quiet gatherings. *True*.

26. I like to take chances. *True*.

27. I enjoy working alone. *True*.

28. Very often a lucky break rather than hard work and persistence, helps a person get ahead. *False.*

* * *

I enjoy reading:

29 Current fiction., *No.*

30. Historical novels. *No.*

31. Classics. *Sometimes.*

32. Biography. *Sometimes.*

33. History. *No.*

34. Poetry. *Sometimes.*

35. Science fiction. *Yes.*

36. Philosophy. *Yes.*

37. Mysteries. *No.*

38. Westerns. *No.*

39. Romance magazines. *No.*

40. Fashion magazines. *Sometimes.*

41. Screen magazines. *No.*

42. Political magazines. *No.*

43. General popular magazines. *Sometimes.*

44. Financial magazines. *No.*

45. Travel books. *No.*

* * *

I enjoy listening to:

46. Symphonic music. *Sometimes.*

47. Rock & Roll. *Yes.*

48. Big beat. *No.*

49. Dixieland. *Sometimes.*

50. Jazz. *Sometimes.*

51. Swing. *No.*

52. Country. *No.*

53. Folk. *No.*

54. Show music. *No.*

55. Opera. *No.*

*   *   *

I enjoy watching or participating in the following kinds of dance:

56. Discotheque. *Yes.*

57. Ballroom. *No.*

58. Latin. *No.*

59. Folk. *No.*

60. Ballet (classical). *Yes.*

61. Ballet (modern). *Yes.*

*   *   *

I am interested in the following kinds of art:

62. Representational paintings. *Yes.*

63. Impressionist paintings. *Yes.*

64. Expressionist paintings. *Yes.*

65. Abstract painting. *Yes.*

66 Ethnic sculpture. *Yes.*

67. Abstract sculpture. *Yes.*

68. Impressionist sculpture. *Yes.*

69 Collage. *Yes.*

70. Construction. *Yes.*

*   *   *

I enjoy:

71. Chess. *No.*

82. Dinner. *Yes.*

72. Bridge. *No.*

73. Poker. *No.*

74. Coin-collecting. *No.*

75. Stamp collecting. *No.*

76. Broadway drama. *No.*

77. Musical comedy. *No.*

78. Watching TV. *Yes.*

79. Travelling in the U.S. *Yes.*

80. Travelling in Europe. *Yes.*

81. Travelling in Asia. *Yes.*

83. Conversation. *Yes.*

84. Movie comedy. *Yes.*

85. Movie drama. *Yes.*

86. Movie musicals. *Yes.*

87. Foreign films. *Yes.*

88. Avant-garde films. *Yes.*

89. Happenings. *Yes.*

90. Off-Broadway plays. *Yes.*

91. Poetry readings. *No.*

92. Museums. *Yes.*

Scramble

a(15),a(72),a(96),a(139),a(145),a(153),ago(40),ago(54),
ago(107),ago(122),all(10),all(46),ambulance(90),and(6),
and(27),and(45),and(51),and(66),and(112),and(119),and
(141),and(147),armies(101),as(59),as(61),as (127),as(129),
attic(69),become(103),bedroom(16),bikes(82),bright(60),
but(33),but(83),but(152),campsites(80),can't(35),can't
(85),can't(157),completely(75),continues(94),covered(17),
different(97),discover(152),errors(49),find(14),find(21),
find(36),find(71),find(78),find(86),find(138),find(158),
foolish(88),forty(38),forty(52),forty(105),forty(120),
furniture(24),haste(91),have(30),have(102),heart(150),
hideous(26),house(3),I(29),in(67),in(95),in(142),in(148),
inside(134),invisible(104),is(4),is(25),just(58),just
(126),life(136),lungs(144),map(74),me(37),me(159),mirror
(154),more(116),moss(19),my(2),my(23),my(41),my(48),my
(108),my(113),my(135),my(143),my(149),named(44),no(31),
now(65),now(133),of(47),once(115),peace(42),place(98),
poisoned(111),postponed(118),proscribed(50),raped(5),
road(73),rooms(12),search(8),seems(64),seems(132),several
(79),several(81),sun(56),sun(63),sun(124),sun(131),taste
(32),that(22),that(28),the(11),the(55),the(62),the(68),
the(92),the(100),the(123),the(130),they(7),they(13),they
(34),they(703),they(77),they(84),they(137),they(151),they
(156),through(9),traffic(88),tree(146),unmarked(76),war
(93),was(43),was(57),was(110),was(117),was(125),weapon
(140),well(109),when(1),wisdom(114),with(18),years(39),
year(53),years(106),years(121),

Measurements

```
from head to toe ...................................5 feet, 10 inches
circumference of head...............................34 inches
nose length .........................................2½ inches
distance between eyes..............................1½ inches
width of mouth......................................3 inches
circumference of neck..............................14½ inches
from shoulder to shoulder..........................19 inches
from  shoulder to elbow.............................11 inches
from elbow to wrist.................................12 inches
circumference of upper arm.........................11 inches
upper  arm flexed..................................13½ inches
circumference of forearm at widest part.............11 inches
circumference of chest at nipples..................37 inches
chest expanded ....................................39 inches
from nipples to navel..............................9 inches
waist at smallest part.............................33 inches
from navel to base of penis........................8 inches
length of penis ...................................3½ inches
erect  penis.......................................6½ inches
circumference of testicals.........................8 inches
distance from testicals to anus....................3 inches
hips at largest part...............................37½ inches
from hip to knee...................................18 inches
from knee to ankle.................................17 inches
circumference of thigh.............................20 inches
circumference of knee..............................15 inches
circumference of calf .............................20 inches
from heel to toe...................................10½ inches
```

CURRENT EVENTS

Film Poem

A film first shown at the Architectural League of New York on January 24, 1968, as part of a series of four poetry events.

Each word——black against a white ground———is a single shot, lasting from three to five seconds. A white blank is inserted between each word (two seconds) so that the words appear as single entities rather than as evolving into each other.

The sound consists of Chinese New Year's street music (gongs, drums, firecrackers) repeated over and over again.

As originally presented, each section was followed by darkness and a taped reading of a short poem.

PART ONE

sky / dwarfs / map / the / hand / in / dotted / hold / ups / blank /
sky / dwarfs / map / the / hand / in / dotted / hold / ups / blank /
but / sharp / to / the / touch / of / movies / or / tickets / booths /
the / both / of / them / were / frozen / refusing / to / look / at /
the / dead / horse / that / broke / the / house / into / separate /
places /
it / was / a / long / way / off / and / it / was / the / width /
of / a / close / up /

it / was / as / if / there / were / a / film / of / vanilla / scented

blue / tinted / liquid / covering / every / thing / and / in / the /
name / of / safety / hiding / it /

to / poke / a hole / in / this / screen / he / fell / asleep /

Short section from BATMEN OF AFRICA,
showing lions and Clyde Beatty.

he / fell / into / a / turmoil / of / images / and / photos /
his / mind / was / a / camera / and / the / film / in / this / camera

was / a / list / of / words/

visible / hand / stands / are / able / to /shake / the / melt /
to / climb / to / film / to / film / to / code / to / bleed (RED)/
I / break / the / film / I / film / the / hunch /

this / film / is / a / message / an / order / a / message / in /
code / an / order / to / see /

the / odor / of / a / dead / horse / the / odor / of / pine / of

film / the /odor / of / words /

       (Red.....Then shot of myself stripped to the
       waist filming myself in a mirror.)

PART TWO

From BATMEN OF AFRICA:

Still of Dagna———
—   "Dagna, High Priest, secretly plans to become
     supreme ruler of Joba through foul means."

Still of Valerie———
     "Valerie brought to Joba by Dagna learns that he
     means to slay her brother."

Still of Gorn———
     "Gorn, keeper of the laws, tells Valerie she can
     thwart Dagna by leaping from the summit of Pinnacle
     Rock:"

Still of Daru———
"Daru, Valerie's brother, is fighting overwhelming odds
in attempting to rescue his sister."

PART THREE

no / one / is / here / no / one / is / here / no / one / is / here /

PART FOUR
(Gold fish . . .)

drive / your / cart / and / your / plough / over / the / bones / of /
the / dead / said / Blake /

what / rough / beast / its / hour / come / round / at / last / slouches /
towards / Bethlehem / to / be / born / ? / asked / Yeats /

no / one / is / drowning / in / the / beautiful / lake / says /
Jon / Lucas /
Who / is / Jon / Lucas / ? /

PART FIVE (RED)

the / odor / of / a / dancer / of / a / film / the /
/ odor / of / a /
dead / horse / breaks / through / the / screen / door / and / causes /
the / balance / to / shift / his / mind / was / a / blank / his / mind /
was / a / screen / it / was / as / if / a / film
/ of / water /
covered / every / thing / making / it / shine /

PART SIX

no/one/is/drowning /in/the / beautiful / lake / no / one / on /
loan / is / sky / drowning / root / one / who / no / in / go / in
no / the / horse / even / beautiful / also / under / to / in /
for / under / leak / lake / also / kite / even /

the-odor-of-a-dead-horse-breaks-thru-the-screen-door-and-causes-the
balance-to-shift-

my / mind / is / a / blank / my / mind / is / a / screen / no / one /
is / here / this / is / a / movie /

no / one / is / drowning / in / the / beautiful / lake /
                                        Face, red etc . . . .)
Flight of the Batmen and destruction of Joba . . . mobs,panic,collapsing
columns, rocks, etc.
                    "The evil are destroyed."

THE END

Balloon

note: Presented as a Poetry Event at Robert Rauschenberg's loft, the evening of May 25, 1968, as part of a series of poetry readings in celebration of the publication of *The Young American Poets,* Follet/ Big Table.

All words and music were pre-recorded on stereo-tape.

1,   "Eye" decals were passed out to members of the audience who were instructed to affix them to their foreheads. Since there was no seating, the audience stood or sat wherever convenient.

2.   Chinese New Year Street Music........4 min.

Sound Effects, Vol. 2, Audio Fidelity DFS 7010.
Drums, gongs, firecrackers, etc, the same one minute cut repeated over and over again.

> ("Plenty of action here, with fervent gongs and drums and bursting firecrackers providing an authentic backdrop for the enthusiasm of both children and adults.")

3.   So as I was saying to you
yesterday,
this rainy season (October)
is very good for mahogany
lumber.
So too is the snow season.

Your lap, however,
disappears when you stand up
to wave goodbye
to the afternoon as it sinks
into the ocean.

Today I am the tomorrow
of your longitude.

And Wednesday I shall be
the road that covers
your stove, your dove,
your smile.

Balloon ? He (you) watches
the balloon
rise up.
First it is balloon-size
and then beachball, basketball,
baseball-size,
an then it is the size of a green pea.

The sky becomes a bowl of soup,
becomes something else
to be looked upon at leisure
with great pleasure.

Is it you? Is it you (me)
that I spot through my range-finder
coming down Main Street,
grinning from ear to ear?

No. It is only the dog of your
Irish sea captain,
foaming.

No. It is only the sunlight
hitting the gas truck
rear-view mirror
as it turns to the right on
Elm Street.

4. The long poem you are about to hear is an acrostic made from the
first two stanzas of the poem you have just heard.

This Poetry Event is entitled *BALLOON* and it is dedicated to the
French artist Odilon Redon who once wrote: "For the most part,
the artists of my generation have looked at a chimney flue and seen
————only a chimney flue. They were not able to give a blank wall
anything of their own essential imagination... Everything that

lent itself to symbolism or that allowed for the unforeseen, the imprecise, the indefinible whose aspect was confused with the enigmatic, led them astray: they were afraid. True parasites of the object, they cultivated art on a purely visual plane....We must remember that we have other things than the eyes to satisfy."

5.   Inflation of a 10 foot weather balloon with helium. The balloon, attached to the helium capsule (bright orange), by fishing tackle, was floated a little more than half way up the three-storey high "chapel" loft. A spot-light illuminated it from below.

6.   *SO AS I WAS SAYING TO YOU*

Springboard into the grassy or the finite
opens the door to the door
as dawn closes another black window
so that light can't move
inside the glassy or the small gray box.

Weather decides. Then as now, we entered,
as always, the present indicative,
stringing along with fourth-string runs on
someone else's sonata machine.

Again the weather. Again the trial balloon.
You plummet. I fold.
Inside the concept "time" as opposed to
nighttime or "perception"
going on and on in spite of the poor reception
the morning or the evening
oozes out of several obscure letters of the alphabet.

Your whisper obscenities into my good ear
often in code so that no one can
understand the decisions, the boycott.

YESTERDAY THIS RAINY SEASON

You come to the parting of ways by way of
eating habits that are invisible
softly with the softness of soft air
to all the incumberances
recalcitrant or redundant
dangerous to pass or to touch.

And then, of course, the passionate way of handling this,
your daydream, is
to make the ambush bulletproof,
however conspicuous, no matter how
isolated from the up-draught.

So stop these rainy days that
release such hopelessness upon
another dry gathering of astronomy buffs.

I can't stand alimony or money problems
nor can I stand
your ability to smile
softly at whatever displeases you.

Enough! And, by the way,
another gripe: your
old-fashioned way of conducting my life,
not by telegrams but by touch.

OCTOBER

(Open the door that leads to the door,
collide with the collision.
That these cartoons are religious
or political
belittles only the incision.
Ergo: the juicy or the crumb;
Reality, however is not so humble.)

IS VERY GOOD FOR THE MAHOGANY LUMBER

I confess to your accusation concerning my
something or other
valuable or invaluable to someone
equally vague
regardless of the Xerox copies
you were kind enough to send me

Gap. We'll close it with a question. The
opening of the clear light
otherwise known as the sphere or the
"dying"
for whatever it is worth. Perhaps nothing
or perhaps
reality in one of its many
theatrical disguises.

Home is where these incongruities relax,
enjoying the unmitigated thrill of
magic tempered by visibility.
Again the perogatives mount. And again
harm becomes vigorous————
————occasionally it also becomes
gamey, sarcastic, trivial, or
alchemical————
Never again. And then again
you become
lackadaisical in your devotions
under financial duress.

My father dies. My mother follows and so do I
being here now but also
elsewhere
remembering the sphere.

SO TOO IS THE SNOW SEASON

Someone, something, somewhere
opens the door to the door
that leads to still yet another door.
Opening or closing. Opening.
Opening the door to the door.

Something moves. It moves into the smoothness of
nothing that spans the remoteness
of your silence that is physical.

We plunge, Into what? Into this
sadness of infinity. This
endless proximity
and then another movement starts
so wordlessly
opening the door to the door,
narrowing time.

YOUR LAP, HOWEVER

Your leap, however,
occupies the stiff territory
under the skin
Repeat: your leap, however,
liquidates the far reaches of the clear
air that is
pornographically blue.

Helicopters cut the line
of least resistance, cut
world message units into
evil images of evil
variously aligned in terms of
evil alignments
removed from the species.

DISAPPEARS WHEN YOU STAND UP

Delight in the sounds of these vowel sounds
inside the circular
stopgap of these visual toys
attentively
prepared towards non-visual ends.

Power circulates
eclipsing the flood
and eclipsing the orb, the eye, the
religion that acts to disguise
someone, something, somewhere else.

We float. We please. We
harm the complete
negotiation that is unpopular.

You————all by yourself————are responsible for
oceans that are dry,
umbrellas that are
so fragile
that they cause more rain
and color the landscape
narrow regions of a singular green.

Decisions to desist
uphold the decision to
prepare for the miraculous inflation.

TO WAVE GOODBYE TO THE AFTERNOON

Tough. It's too bad that logic is
often impractical in dealing
with the contingencies, the
announcements that arrive in the form of
vehicles of remorse
endlessly verbose

Gaining this insight is a loss to the world
of business and/or publicity
oddities that
depend upon
biology or chemistry.
You told me this and I agreed
eventually
that the eyes have it
over the ears:
that the mind is hollow,
ending the synapse.

Again the moment is
folded up into
tiny pieces
each irregular in shape
repeating the eylids of the grammar.

Now is the time
our endlessness is discreet,
our pleasures are concealed
not only by the visual.

AS IT SINKS INTO THE OCEAN

Aimless wanderings. Aimless sludge.
Stomach pumps.
Instant crime. I bow out.

The words become interiorized.
Society melts
into a large pool that
narrows down the birth rate and
kindness becomes agressive.

Sleep. Sleep that
imaginary boundary of dreams
needs some air raid sirens

to keep these windows from
humming mindlessly into the
eye of the stupidity.

Oceanography becomes
contemplative.
Eyes see only the verbalized
and then when the fire begins
nothingness becomes tangible.

7. Thank you for your cooperation and your attention ... Please remove your "eyes."

8. Black out. Chinese New Year Street Music, while balloon is pulled
down and deflated in the darkness. Lights.

THE END

Alternatives

First performance: Central Park Poetry
Events, The Band Shell On The Mall, N.Y.C.
September 29, 1968.

There are five separate information sources————three visual and two
audio. Each member of the audience is free to choose one source or several sources upon which to focus his attention. Most of the "information"
is repeated several times throughout the piece. Each person will hear or
see different messages, depending upon his attentiveness and his psycho-
logical pre-disposition.

The visual information sources consist of three trays of 80 slides each,
rear-projected upon separate but adjoining screens at a speed of five
seconds per slide. Kodak Carousel slide projectors are employed so that
each tray is repeated over and over again automatically. Single words
in each set (tray) when viewed and understood in succession create grammatical sentences in an aural (one word at a time) mode rather than in
a visual (linear) mode. The three sets viewed simultaneously create a logical, non-syntactical juxtaposition of words, creating a fugal effect.

I am interested in "reading" and in controlling reading speed.

The aural information sources are created by a stereo tape. One word
heard on the left is followed by another unrelated word heard on the
right. It is possible to listen to both tracks simultaneously, but if one
listens to only those words on the right or the left seperately, grammatical sentences will be perceived.

I am interested in psycholinguistics and "The Coctail Party Problem"
(i.e. given several sources of information, how are we able to separate
out one source from other sources?).

Directional separations are indicated in the text (IV & V) by the capi-
talization of all those words heard on the left and the use of lower case
for words heard on the right. Visual sources (I,II,III) and aural sources
(IV & V) operate simultaneously and continuously.

188

Structure: Since all sets of information are repeated and can be repeated endlessly, the piece is potentially endless. Beginning and ending are arbitrary. In the Central Park presentation the piece was stopped after twenty-five minutes, but it could have continued for any length of time.

I am interested in making "poetry" in an indirect way. The text (literature) is a bi-product generated by the event, rather than the other way around.

Visual:			Audio:
I	II	III	IV (left) & v (right)
screen	the	to	Once THEY and WENT for TO all CENTRAL i
out	breaks	slide	PARK have AND to STOPPED tell AT you THE
all	day	down	the BAND whole SHELL truth IT about WAS
the	into	hills	the AFTER matter NOON. we IT have WAS
noises	many	that	been A considering SUNNY not SEPTEMBER
that	gray	don't	for DAY one BUT moment THERE believing
are	pieces	exist	WAS that NO you ONE will ELSE believe
green	8	is	AROUND. me SHE Here TOOK is OFF a HER
or	and	flat	piece CLOTHES of AND my DID mind. A here
are	then	10	LITTLE is DANCE X a ON screen THE or
signals	on	and	STAGE . a HE series FOLLOWED of HER.
to	his	then	screens SUDDENLY upon A which LARGE you
your	break	I	DOG may APPEARED or INSIDE may THE not
skin	he	marry	HEAD OF project THE your STATUE lack
of	goes	you	OF of LIBERTY desire. SUDDENLY The
dreams	to	by	THERE sea WAS shell AN ACCIDENT you AT
17	work	proxy,	discoverd FIFTH on AVENUE you AND
stones,	on	eating	summer FORTY vacation SECOND is STREET.
rocks,	the	my	missing. A The WOMAN publicity IN is
trees,	climax	cake	HER here. FORTIES Stones ATE shaped
grass,	21	and	A like GUN. doenuts. SHE Rocks THOUGHT
cars,	the	halfing	as SHE soft NEW as HIM butter. BETTER
faces,	kite	it.	Trees THAN made ANY of ONE fiberglasss.
clouds,	fails	24	ELSE cars ALIVE. made SHE of WAS soft
all	25	to	WRONG. ice YOU cream. CAME Faces HOME
keep	this	calf	made FROM to WORK love. AND Clouds
their	park	is	SURPRISED to THEM. buy................
special	without	to	....

places	trees	dream
in	flees	of
spite	the	you
of	city	32
the	for	I
scramble	some	crash
for	other	35
more	place	I
dark	where	slide
choices	the	into
39	climate	the
five	is	green
kinds	blue	debris
of	and	that
action	where	makes
cause	the	a
a	day	fool
reaction	begins	of
either	without	me
one	a	by
by	sound	becoming
one	50	too
or	my	solid
all	wrists	52
together	are	our
54	bound	life
and	55	is
then	he	a
buy	breaks	stage
take	into	that
a	many	brings
full	gray	us
grown	pieces	one
lake	inside	step
with	the	closer
boats	band	to
in	shell	your
it	66	laugh
and	the	7

THEY all WENT of TO a CENTRAL sudden PARK i AND fell STOPPED stilly. AT i THE feel BAND trapped SHELL. inside IT these WAS screens. AFTER the NOON. damp IT night WAS air A is SUNNY responsible SEPTEMBER for DAY this BUT clear THERE cut WAS case NO of ONE self ELSE indulgence. AROUND. Someone SHE somewhere TOOK is OFF dying HER this CLOTHES very AND minute. DID i A know LITTLE about DANCE dying. ON Just THE as STAGE. much HE as FOLLOWED the HER. next SUDDENLY guy, A maybe LARGE more. DOG we APPEAR-ED fool INSIDE our THE selves HEAD into OF believing THE we STATUE are OF really LIBERTY. here, THERE all WAS in AN one ACCIDENT piece, ON all FIFTH in AVENUE one AND place. FORTY You SECOND and STREET. i A know WOMAN better. In we HER can FORTIES divide ATE our A selves GUN. up SHE into THOUGHT tautologies. SHE But KNEW to HIM slide BETTER down THAN imaginary ANY hills ONE is ELSE too ALIVE. personal. SHE The WAS best WRONG. of YOU us CAME would HOME rather FROM upon WORK candy AND stores SURPRISED for THEM. you ....
ONCE all AND of FOR a ALL sudden I i HAVE feel TO silly. TELL i YOU feel THE trapped WHOLE inside TRUTH these ABOUT screens. THE the MATTER damp WE night HAVE air BEEN is CONSIDERING, responsible NOT for FOR this ONE clear MOMENT cut BELIEVING case THAT of YOU self WILL indulgence. BE-LIEVE Someone ME. somewhere HERE is IS dying A this PIECE very OF minute. MY i MIND. know HERE about IS dying. A Just SCREEN as OR much A as SERIES the OF next SCREENS guy, UPON maybe WHICH more. YOU we MAY

move
it
out
of
reach
73
cities
fall
from
where
they
die
80
screen
out
all
the
noises
that
are
green
or
are
signals
to
your
skin
of
dreams
17
stones,
rocks,
trees,
grass,
cars,
faces,
clouds,
all
keep

band
shell
breaks
up
into
many
gray
pieces
76
the
trees
die
80

the
day
breaks
into
many
gray
pieces
8
and
then
on
his
break
he
goes
to
work
on
the
climax
21
the
kite
fails
25

I
take
these
things
in
my
stride

74
I
eat
my
wounded
bride
80

to
slide
down
hills
that
don't
exist
is
flat
10
and
then
I
marry
you
by
proxy,
eating
my
cake
and
halfing
it.

fool OR our MAY selves NOT into
PROJECT believing YOUR we LACK are OF
really DESIRE. here, THE all SEA in SHELL
one YOU piece, DISCOVERED all ON in YOUR
one SUMMER place. VACATION You IS and
MISSING i THE know PUBLICITY better. IS
we HERE. can STONES divide SHAPED our LIE
selves DOENUTS. up ROCKS into AS
tautologies. SOFT But AS to BUTTER. slide
TREES down MADE imaginary OF hills
FIBERGLASS. is CARS too MADE personal
OF The SOFT best ICE of CREAM. us FACES
would MADE rather TO open LOVE. candy
CLOUDS stores TO for BUY. you..............
....

ALL to OF park A the SUDDEN car. I to
FEEL elevate. SILLY. to I carve FEEL
the TRAPPED park INSIDE into THESE
jealous SCREENS. pieces. THE to DAMP be
NIGHT all AIR of IS one RESPONSIBLE piece.
FOR to THIS be CLEAR responsible CUT
for CASE yourself. OF to SELF vanish INDUL-
GENCE. into SOMEONE thin SOMEWHERE
air. IS to DYING die THIS without VERY
leaving MINUTE. a I trace. KNOW to ABOUT
converse. DYING, to JUST find AS new
MUCH friends AS and THE to NEXT regain
GUY. old MAYBE ones MORE. you WE haven't
FOOL seen OUR in SELVES a INTO long
BELIEVING time. We to ARE change REALLY
your HERE name ALL and IN become ONE a
PIECE new ALL person. IN to ONE slide.
PLACE. to YOU tape. AND to I record
KNOW the BETTER. distance WE from CAN
one DIVIDE place OUR to SELVES another.
UP to INTO jump TAUTOLOGIES. the BUT gun.
TO to SLIDE marry DOWN someone IMAGIN-
ARY by HILLS proxy. IS to TOO fly PERSONAL
a THE kite BEST on OF a US nice WOULD

their
special
places
in
spite
of
the
scramble
for
more
dark
choices
39
five
kinds
of
action
cause
a
reaction
either
one
by
one
or
all
together
54
and
then
you

this
park
without
trees
flees
the
city
for
some
other
place
where
the
climate
is
blue
and
where
the
day
begins
without
a
sound
50
my
wrists
are
bound
55
he

24.
to
calf
is
to
dream
of
you
32
I
crash
35
I
slide
into
the
green
debris
that
makes
a
fool
of
me
by
becoming
too
solid
52
our
life

September RATHER after OPEN noon.
CANDY to STORES make FOR no YOU
appearances ....
to THEY park WERE the MARRIED car. LAST
to SPRING elevate. AND to ALREADY carve
THEY the ARE park SEPARATED into AND
jealous NO pieces. LONGER to THINK be
OF all ONE of ANOTHER one THE piece.
SQUIRREL to BEGGED be FOR responsible
FOOD for BUT yourself. THEY to WERE
vanish BUSY into MAKING thin LOVE. air.
THEY to WERE die BUSY without ARGUING.
leaving INSIDE a THE trace. to HEAD
converse. OF to THE find STATUE new OF
friends LIBERTY and TWO to TEENAGERS
regain WERE old MAKING ones LOVE. you
HE haven't PUSHED seen HER in OVER a
THE long EDGE time. OF to THE change
BAND your SHELL. name HE and BEGAN
become TO a SLIDE new INTO person. HIS
to OLD slide. HABITS. to TWO tape.
BICYCLES to COLLIDED. record BUT the
THIS distance TIME from AROUND one NO
place ONE to WAS another. HURT. to
THERE jump WERE the NO gun. CHILDREN to
INVOLVED. marry someone HIS by VACATION
proxy. WAS to OVER. fly HIS a WRIST
kite FELL on OFF. a ABOVE nice THE
September PARK after AN noon. AIRPLANE
to MOVED make THROUGH no CLOUDS
appearances........................

(etc.)

Whisper

First performed at Robert Rauschenberg's loft on May 25, 1968.

During any social event or gathering, without making any announcement, whisper into the ears of as many people as possible the following one line poem:

"No one is drowning in the beautiful lake."

Whisper (Second Version):
You Never Know What's Going to Happen Next

First performed at the Orient Expresso
Coffee House on November 5, 1968.

The performer places a small portable radio on a table in front of the audience and announces the full title of the event. He turns the radio on and tunes it to station WINS, a station in New York City that offers continuous news and has as one of its advertising slogans the phrase: You never know what's going to happen next.

If this event is to be performed outside the range of this particular radio station, any other similar station will do or a tape recording of several of the day's news reports can be substituted.

Performer then moves down into the audience and whispers one word of the slogan to one person at a time.

First person hears: You
Second person hears: Never
Third person hears: Know
Etc.

The slogan is repeated over and over again, one word at a time, until every person in the audience has heard one word.

If the audience is of such a size that the whole process will take more than fifteen minutes, more than one performer may be used.

Bicycle Street Event

First performed on West 26th Street,
August 1968.

Performer, stripped to the waist with the word "life" on his back, wearing a gas mask, wheels a bicycle down the length of a city block. Concealed in a pouch on the bicycle is a small portable tape recorder which is playing a tape of the following words repeated over and over again:

"By noon the town was closed.
I borrowed some additional clothes and
cycled to the outpost.
You bordered upon hysteria and were
closer to reality than I,
lacking only the cleverness I need
each time something goes wrong."

Letter Event

First performed on January 2, 1969.

Send letters to fifty people chosen at random from the telephone book. The letters should be typed and there should be no return address or signature. The letter should read:

"Your name has been chosen at random from the telephone book."

Matches

First performed at the Orient Expresso
Coffee House on November 5, 1968.

Darken the performance area.

Light a match and then blow it out.

Continue doing this until all twenty matches
from a book of safety matches
have been lit and then extinguished.

Tape Event

First performed at the Longview Country
Club, November 17, 1968.

Using masking tape, make a large X on every window in the room or
auditorium in which this piece is performed.

Rainbow

First performed at the Orient Expresso Coffee House, on November 5, 1968.

Performer: I will now say the word "rainbow" to myself fifty times.

Performer stands or sits perfectly still and says the word "rainbow" to himself.

Note: Other possibilities include *not* saying the word "rainbow" fifty times or saying it 100 times or saying another word, etc.

Performer: I have now said the word "rainbow" to myself fifty times.

(Did the performer really say the word "rainbow" fifty times? How do you know? Did you believe him when he said that he would do this and then when he said that he had done it? Why or why not?

A note on the author: John Perreault was born in New York City in 1937. He is the art critic for the Village Voice and an Editorial Associate of Art News. His first book of poems, *Camouflage*, was published by Lines Press in 1966.